# NIETZSCHE
# IN THE EARLY WORK OF
# THOMAS MANN

BY
R. A. NICHOLLS

UNIVERSITY OF CALIFORNIA PRESS
BERKELEY AND LOS ANGELES
1955

University of California Publications in Modern Philology
Editors (Berkeley): A. H. Rowbotham, C. G. Loomis, E. S. Morby, Gleb Struve

University of California Press
Berkeley and Los Angeles
California

❖

Cambridge University Press
London, England

# PREFACE

I AM VERY PLEASED to have the opportunity to express here my gratitude and appreciation to Professor Hans M. Wolff of the Department of German at the University of California, Berkeley. It was at his suggestion that this work was undertaken, and I am in debt to him for his constant assistance and encouragement.

I want also to thank many other members of the staff of the University of California, especially Professors Marianne Bonwit, Andrew O. Jaszi, and Karl Aschenbrenner for their guidance and help.

I am greatly obliged to Alfred A. Knopf, Inc., of New York for freely granting me permission to make use of their editions of Thomas Mann's works in translation, and also to Mrs. Maud Rosenthal of Oxford, England, for her kind permission to quote extensively from the translations of the works of Friedrich Nietzsche, edited by Oscar Levy, and published by T. N. Foulis & Co., Edinburgh.

# CONTENTS

# I. INTRODUCTION

THOMAS MANN has frequently emphasized the important part Nietzsche played in the early development of his work. On two occasions Mann has discussed at length the extent and significance of his Nietzsche studies: first in the *Observations of a Nonpolitical Man,* when under the stress of the First World War he examined the background and origins of his career; and then again in the *Sketch of My Life,* a study made when he was awarded the Nobel prize for literature in 1929. In both essays Mann attempted a broad assessment of the essential influence Nietzsche had exerted on the whole pattern of his work and thought. Criticism has accepted Mann's lead, but the implications of Nietzsche's influence have been discussed only in general terms, either as part of an examination of the background of Mann's thought or in an estimate of Mann's place in literary history. Although the importance of this influence is generally recognized, no attempt has been made to examine in detail the extent to which this influence is directly reflected in Mann's writings. The object of my study is rather to analyze the early works from the point of view of their Nietzschean content. It aims to show the extent to which the problems and conflicts with which Mann deals are understood in Nietzschean terms. It will show Mann's constant, often concealed, use of Nietzschean symbols and phraseology, and will examine how this usage reflects a very close sympathy and relationship in their outlook on the world. This study is not simply one of an external influence, but leads into the very heart of Mann's work.

The young Thomas Mann remained isolated from contemporary intellectual movements. His sense of separateness was such that even in Munich he made few contacts with artistic and literary groups. The distaste he felt for the facile convictions of the progressive men of letters, the "Zivilisationsliteraten," as he later called them in the *Observations of a Nonpolitical Man,* must have kept him apart from the dominant intellectual circles to which his brother Heinrich Mann belonged. At the same time, neither the aestheticism of the Stefan George circle and the other exponents of "l'art pour l'art" nor dogmatic naturalism, which still had active support, could hold an appeal for him. On the one hand, he must have felt little understanding for the indifference of the aestheticist group to the ethical problems that were his own deepest concern; on the other hand, however much he may have owed to naturalist technique, especially in *Buddenbrooks,* the naturalist search for absolute truthfulness in the representation of life must have seemed very doubtful to a man so skeptical of the motives of the artist as Mann showed himself to be.

In this isolation from significant literary contacts, Mann turned with correspondingly greater enthusiasm to other guides with whom he felt a natural affinity. It was the triumvirate Schopenhauer, Wagner, Nietzsche—"the trinity of eternally united spirits," as he called them in the *Observations*—that became the basis of his artistic and intellectual development. Critics have emphasized the difficulty of distinguishing the influence these three men exercised on Thomas Mann.[1] Mann himself says in the *Observations of a Nonpolitical Man*[2] that he found it impossible to separate what he learned from each of them. The same "ethical atmosphere," in Nietzsche's phrase, prevails in all three—the same spiritual mood that dominated Mann's own early life and work.

It was, however, Nietzsche as critic who interpreted this mood and its significance to Mann. In his *Sketch of My Life* Mann makes a clear distinction between the particular character of Nietzsche's influence and that of the others. The Nietzschean influence, he says, was intellectual and artistic; Schopenhauer's influence was spiritual.[3] Reading Schopenhauer, he argues, was like a metaphysical intoxication for him; it was a "passionate, almost a mystical experience," rather than a truly philosophical one. Although Schopenhauer put into words much of Mann's own longing, the actual doctrine of Schopenhauer's work—the Buddhistic, ascetic conquest of the will—was irrelevant and had no meaning for Mann. On the contrary, he associates the emotions that the work arouse—"sensual, more than sensual"—with the erotic, most unascetic music of Wagner's *Tristan*. This association of mood he had already stressed in the *Observations* when he discussed the occasion of his first reading of Schopenhauer.

Lonely and irregular youth, with its longing for the world and for death, how it swallowed the magic potion of this metaphysics, whose inmost nature is eroticism and in which I recognized the spiritual source of the Tristan music.[4]

He read Schopenhauer for days and nights together, "as one reads perhaps only once in one's life." Mann causes his early hero Thomas

---

[1] Cf. Carl Helbling, *Die Gestalt des Künstlers in der neueren Dichtung;* Hans Meyer, *Thomas Mann;* Henry Hatfield, *Thomas Mann.*
[2] *Betrachtungen eines Unpolitischen*, p. 37. This book has not been translated. Subsequent references are made to it as *Observations.*
[3] *A Sketch of My Life*, p. 24.
[4] P. 38.

Buddenbrook, at a critical moment in his life, to read Schopenhauer with this same devotion. It was not an intellectual experience, but an emotional one; he did not analyze and discuss, he loved and accepted. He was absorbed entirely, carried away by the power and mastery with which Schopenhauer controlled his theme. And at the time Mann first read Schopenhauer, as he tells us in the *Observations*,[5] his passion for Wagner also reached its peak. Schopenhauer and Wagner expressed for Mann, as it were, different sides of the same experience. Wagner discovered in Schopenhauer's presentation of the world a spirit from which his own work could take form. To Mann, Wagner's music is the accompaniment and fulfillment of Schopenhauer's philosophy.

At the same time, it is important to note Mann's insistence that he studied Schopenhauer and Wagner when he was well aware of Nietzsche's attacks on them. They too had guided Nietzsche to maturity, and he had revolted against them. Mann read Schopenhauer after some acquaintance with Nietzsche's work,[6] and the speed and intensity with which he was able to absorb the earlier philosopher are explained through his study of Nietzsche. Mann read with a love that was conditioned but not weakened by his knowledge of Nietzsche's criticism. It was the same with Wagner, and Mann himself in the *Observations* has tried to explain this point of view in analyzing his relationship to the composer. He describes his feeling as a passion, a devotion made up of intense love, but sharpened by knowledge. The harsh psychological criticism that Nietzsche brought to Wagner's work did not lessen this love. On the contrary, through this criticism and by means of it his love became a true passion, "with all the claims that passion can impose on the nervous tension."[7]

Inwardly the most difficult and most fearful experience of my youth was this, to learn that passion must be clear-sighted, or else is not worthy of its name. Blind love, love that is nothing but a panegyrical apotheosis of the beloved, that is a beautiful illusion.[8]

For this reason Schopenhauer and Wagner are deliberately used by Mann in his early work as symbols of a condition of mind or spiritual atmosphere that he wishes to convey. When Thomas Buddenbrook reads Schopenhauer, for example, it marks a stage in his degeneration. It is an overwhelming experience that has been prepared for by the conditions of his life. Similarly, Hanno Buddenbrook's devo-

[5] P. 39.
[6] Cf. *A Sketch of My Life*, p. 24.
[7] P. 41.
[8] P. 40.

tion to music—above all to Wagner and the late romantics—
symptom of the family's disruption. These are symbols of a
emotional power that Mann uses to heighten his effects. He doe
use Nietzsche in this way; Nietzsche is the critic who had imp
on him an interpretation of the significance and implications of
ner's and Schopenhauer's works. Mann's writing springs fro
knowledge of this criticism; he shares the same emotional reactions
as Nietzsche, the complex of love and revolt that Nietzsche himself
had felt.

It is clear that Mann does not seek in Nietzsche, any more than
he does in Schopenhauer, an objective philosophy from which he may
draw ideas and opinions concerning the nature of man and the universe. He does not turn to philosophy as another field of human knowledge, independent of his own experience or unrelated to his own
needs. He understands Nietzsche's work and life as far as it concerns
him—that is, as a personal struggle with problems and experiences
that were close to his own; he finds his own ideas and his own feelings
more clearly expressed and thought out on a wider plane. He does
not take Nietzsche's extreme doctrines literally. "I believed him hardly
at all," he says in the *Observations*. The immoralist creed, the superman cult, and the ruthless doctrines of power were of no interest to
him in themselves, but were comprehensible only in the context and
conditions of Nietzsche's life. In the course of the present study I
shall show what aspects of Nietzsche's thought and what predominant
themes in Nietzsche's life and work were of importance to Mann. I am
not concerned with a criticism of the validity of such a personal approach to Nietzsche or with examining whether Mann's is a correct
evaluation of the philosophy. What I seek to show is the way in which
Mann makes use of Nietzsche in his works, and how the course and
development of Mann's thought are guided by his sympathetic relationship to Nietzsche. It will, however, appear that it is only because
of this intimate association of feeling that his contact with Nietzsche
was so fruitful to Mann as a creative writer.

As early as Mann's first collection of short stories, published in
1898 under the title *Little Herr Friedemann*, there is some reflection
of his Nietzsche studies. Although the original stimulus for these
stories and for *Buddenbrooks* comes from Mann's own experience,
and Mann deliberately emphasizes the personal element, there is clear
evidence to show that he found essential support in Nietzsche both

for the basis of his judgments and for the consistency of the psychological values by which his characters are interpreted. The importance of this dependence upon Nietzsche becomes clearer in *Tonio Kröger*. Although this work seems the most personal and intimate of all Mann's early writings, it will be seen that the conflicts of Kröger's life are at the same time presented specifically in Nietzschean terms, so that Kröger's confession as an artist has to be interpreted in the light of Nietzsche's thought. In this way the plight of the artist, sick and looking for an inner contact with life, is understood in its widest significance. It is found that Kröger's true task lies in his attempt to establish a basis of moral validity for his work, and this attempt is related to Nietzsche's struggle to maintain a real standard of values in the face of a world become empty of meaning. A study of the other main works written before the first war—*Tristan, Fiorenza, Royal Highness,* and *Death in Venice*—shows Mann's further elaboration of this all-embracing problem in its bearing to the essential Nietzschean premises. The conflict is extended beyond the personal experience of the artist and brought into relation with the whole problem of cultural vitality and decay.

The inquiry ends with the *Observations of a Nonpolitical Man.* In this long and involved essay Mann tries to establish what his own representative place is in the whole tradition of German and European culture, as he stands as a successor to Nietzsche. He wants to estimate how this tradition is reflected in the particular character of his own writings and his own reaction to the world around him. The cultural problems that the war brought into the open, in order to be truly understood, must be related to his own experience. The *Observations* is thus a key work in Mann's career. In extending the implications of his early "personal" writings, he makes clearer the unity and cohesion of his work and brings out the direct relationship between the confessional tales and the universal problems of his later philosophical novels. The themes of the later books are an extension, though along various new lines, of problems raised in the *Observations.* In this essay Nietzsche is of paramount importance. It is only through Nietzsche that he can seek the true explanation of the world crisis. For this reason Mann feels the need to rely on Nietzsche, both inwardly, in understanding his own fate, and outwardly, in the political field. Mann's attacks on what he considers the superficial ideals of the Western Allies and his defense of German values are both founded on Nietzschean argument.

In the later novels the Nietzsche influence is no longer the central factor in interpretation. My inquiry serves as a preparation for understanding Mann's later development, but a valid estimation of these works can no longer be made by a one-sided approach of this kind. Previously it was found that Nietzsche led into the real heart of the work; but now, although it may be argued that Nietzsche provides the background from which Mann begins, and—at least in *Dr. Faustus*—it is Nietzsche to whom he comes back, the subject matter has been greatly extended. There is a whole wealth of new intellectual influences and interests that must be understood for an interpretation of this development. Mann is more and more consciously writing as a "late-comer" and heir to the whole of man's cultural past.

# II. BEGINNINGS: THE EARLY NOVELLEN AND BUDDENBROOKS

In the *Sketch of My Life* Mann says he was twenty years old when he first came to read Nietzsche.[1] Again, in the *Observations,* he speaks of studying Nietzsche at the age of twenty.[2] These statements are borne out by an examination of the early stories. There are no traces of Nietzsche in the short tale *Fallen*[3] which Mann published in 1894 when he was nineteen. But in *The Will to Happiness,* which followed two years later,[4] there is specific evidence of Mann's contact with the philosopher. Apart from the title, clearly patterned after Nietzsche's *Will to Power,* Mann makes a significant reference here also to the familiar Nietzschean concept of a "pathos of distance" that separates the hero from his fellow students.

Although it was *Fallen,* published by M. G. Conrad in his periodical *Die Gesellschaft,* that first brought Mann to the attention of the literary world and aroused the interest and encouragement of Richard Dehmel, it has for us little of the character of Mann's work as we know it. It is essentially derivative and strongly influenced by contemporary work both in style, with its short, impressionistic sentences, and in subject matter. *Fallen* is a charming, adolescent love story with the not particularly original moral that a girl who one day gives herself for love will later sell herself for money. Although the emphasis on the disillusionment of the man who tells the story is of significance in the later Mann,[5] his development did not follow at all from this beginning. *The Will to Happiness* is a new start. It is only here that, despite the uncertainties of a melodramatic plot, we are clearly present in a world we recognize as Mann's own. It seems that Mann only now came to discover the terms in which he could interpret his own experience. The extent to which Nietzsche contributed to this new basis for his writing can only be conjectured, but the deliberate references indicate the degree of Mann's interest.

Certainly the original impulse for this story does not come from any

---

[1] P. 22.

[2] P. 318.

[3] Published in *Die Gesellschaft,* November, 1894. This story has been neither reprinted nor translated.

[4] Published in *Simplicissimus,* August, 1896. This story was reprinted in the collection entitled *Der kleine Herr Friedemann* (Berlin, 1898), but was not included in the 1922 collection of Novellen or in subsequent editions. It has not been translated into English.

[5] Cf. Hans Meyer's discussion of *Fallen* in his *Thomas Mann* (Berlin, 1950), pp. 15 ff.

outside reading, but, as in all the very early short stories, is to be found in Mann's own psychological experiences and early conflict with the world. The mood, the atmosphere, and the sense of values are the expression of Mann's own most personal reflections. An analysis of the tale helps, however, to show the inner relationship between this personal experience and the guidance Mann found in Nietzsche. It suggests the reason for his early sense of kinship with the philosopher.

In the circumstances of his hero's life Mann, as he was so often to do, reproduces much of his own situation. The name—Paolo Hoffman— like Tonio Kröger, indicates the hero's origins; for whereas his father is a north German businessman of a well-established middle-class family, his mother is of exotic South American blood. This racial mixture symbolizes the conflicts of Paolo's life and explains why he feels unable to find a place among his fellow students. Like Kröger and the other early heroes, Paolo is oversensitive and withdrawn; he has no sense of assurance or self-justification. Certain episodes of his youth—his unreturned love for a girl he meets at a dancing class when he is sixteen, for example—also foreshadow the experience of Tonio Kröger, but the development of the story follows quite different lines.

Paolo is entirely unadapted to the harsh conditions of life. He is sickly, his heart is weak, and his chances of a long life very doubtful. When he falls in love with a girl from an intellectual Munich family, the girl's father will not allow the marriage because of the young man's health. Paolo runs away, travels in Italy and Africa, but then receives a message from the father begging him to return and withdrawing all objections to the match, because his daughter cannot be happy without Paolo. Paolo's heart has become far worse; he can live only with extreme care and circumspection. Indeed only his unfulfilled will to happiness seems to have kept him alive. When he gets the message he travels back at once to Munich, knowing that he is going to his death, but in calm acceptance that this is his destiny. In fact, on the very night after the wedding he dies.

The connections with Nietzsche in this strangely melodramatic story are loose but clearly noticeable. It becomes evident that what first attracts Mann in Nietzsche is the sense of isolation that comes from suffering. Paolo's friend, who is the narrator of the story, describes the origin of their comradeship: "It was that 'pathos of distance' towards the great number of our fellow-students, which everyone knows who at fifteen secretly reads Heine and in lower school makes decisive judgments on the world and on man."⁶ The phrase "pathos of distance" is used by Nietzsche on a number of occasions, but what he means appears most clearly perhaps in the section "What is noble?" in *Beyond Good and Evil.*

Without the *pathos of distance*, such as grows out of the incarnated difference of classes, out of the constant overlooking and downlooking of the ruling caste on subordinates and instruments, and out of their equally constant practice of obeying and commanding, of keeping down and keeping at a distance,—that other more mysterious pathos could never have arisen, the longing for an ever new widening of distance within the soul itself, the formation of ever higher, rarer, further, more extended, more comprehensive states, in short, just the elevation of the type "man." . . .⁷

"Feelings of distance," Nietzsche says, are the *"prerequisite* for every elevation of man."⁸ Again, in discussing what he means by "nobility," Nietzsche finds it in the sense of separation caused through the capacity for suffering. "Profound suffering makes noble; it separates";⁹ and he says: "It almost determines the order of rank how deeply men can suffer."¹⁰

Nietzsche thus gave emphatic support to Mann's youthful pride in standing apart, and provided a justification for his sufferings. It is significant that Mann later described this early pride of isolation in very Nietzschean terms. In the essay "Goethe as a Representative of the Bourgeois Age" Mann speaks of "my youthful notion of aristocracy which quite definitely amounted to a sublime incapacity and lack of vocation for ordinary life."¹¹

This was, however, only one side of the question. *The Will to Happiness* includes the theme that was to become increasingly important in all Mann's stories at this period. Sensitivity and subtlety of feeling and taste are in themselves reckoned as evidence of sickness and degeneracy. The hero is judged in terms of life; he is condemned because he is unable to accept the conditions of life. Paolo's sensitivity and his sickness are two facets of his inner decay. This is the same dominant

---

⁶ *Der kleine Herr Friedmann* (Berlin, 1898), p. 71.

⁷ 12, p. 223. Reference is to *The Complete Works of Friedrich Nietzsche*, edited by Oscar Levy, in eighteen volumes, published by T. N. Foulis and Company, Edinburgh and London, 1909–1913. For the contents of each volume, see Bibliography. The first number cited refers to the corresponding number in the Nietzsche section of the Bibliography.

⁸ 16, p. 186.

⁹ 8, p. 78.

¹⁰ 8, p. 77.

¹¹ *Essays of Three Decades*, p. 83. Copyright 1929, 1933, 1937, 1947 by Alfred A. Knopf, Inc.

motif as in the story of the Buddenbrooks, where a growth of intellectual and artistic gifts is accompanied by a decline in vitality and the power of healthy adaptation to life.

The basis of Paolo's heroism—and here again we feel Mann's youthful interpretation of Nietzsche—is that he affirms life, that in spite of his sickness he asserts his will to the service of life. He freely abandons the idle, meaningless existence of his travels abroad for the sake of a night with his beloved that will mean his death but also the triumph of his deepest instincts. The will to happiness—a very subordinate impulse according to Nietzsche—is in fact the will to life itself, which must be satisfied though it kills its possessor.

In spite of the many extravagant features of this story, we already find ourselves in the representative mood and atmosphere of Mann's early work. After this there is no more hesitation in his choice of subject and theme. In the next two stories, *Little Herr Friedemann* and *The Dilettante,* the longest and most carefully worked out of his very earliest tales, the problems remain the same, though they are presented with more confidence and without romantic intrusions.

The hero in each is again an outcast, separated by his sensitivity from the society of his fellows. He attempts to create a life of his own that will serve to keep away the demands of the outer world; he makes an uneasy escape into literature and art and the realms of the imagination. Each time he is condemned.

In *Friedemann* a physical disability accounts for the hero's isolation. Injured as a baby, he grows up a hunchback, unable to take part in the games and activities of his companions. Later he finds himself equally excluded from the passions and loves that govern their lives. Forced to limit himself, he seeks instead to train with minute care his capacity for an aesthetic enjoyment of what life still has to offer. And in this he seems to achieve a certain success. His life passes comfortably, and when he is thirty he is able to say: "Well, so that is thirty years. Perhaps there may be ten or even twenty more, God knows. . . . I look forward to them with peace in my heart."[12]

This peace is illusory. He comes to lose the scrupulous control of his feelings, and is overwhelmed by an outburst of passion. He tries to resist the power of the woman who has attracted him, but gives way. All the barriers behind which he tried to find contentment are destroyed. As he sits on the bank of the river with the woman he loves,

---

[12] *Stories of Three Decades,* p. 7. Copyright 1930, 1931, 1934, 1935, 1936 by Alfred A. Knopf, Inc. Subsequently cited as *Stories.*

she asks him if he has been happy during these thirty years. And he replies: "I tried to be happy ..., but that was all lies and imagination."[13] As in *The Will to Happiness,* the story ends in violent drama. When she rejects his love, as he knows she will, he is crushed by a sense of uncontrollable disgust with himself and sinks down into the river.

Friedemann had set himself the task of training his capacity for enjoyment, of learning to appreciate all experiences; he had loved music and had come to acquire a subtle taste for literature. "He knew how to savour the seductive rhythm of a lyric or the ultimate flavour of a subtly told tale—yes one might almost call him a connoisseur."[14]

In the original the term used is "Epikuräer," and it is interesting that this Epicurean ideal to which Friedemann subscribes is an important symbol in Nietzsche's work and a symbol used in very much the same way as Mann uses it here. Epicureanism has as its ideal the avoidance of pain and suffering. In Nietzsche's interpretation: "To seek happiness would be nonsense, that would mean seeking something negative! But to avoid suffering, that is the aim."[15] Such an ideal, he says, is essentially decadent. "Epicurus was a typical decadent; I was the first to recognize him as such." And he goes on: "The terror of pain, even of infinitely slight pain, such a state cannot possibly help culminating in a *religion* of love."[16] He frequently suggests a relationship between Epicureanism and the Christian religion of the weak. Epicureanism is in fact "the doctrine of redemption of paganism." On another occasion Nietzsche says that Epicurus is the antagonist of the Dionysian Greek, where Dionysus is the being richest in overflowing vitality. Epicurus, in effect, plays the same role as Schopenhauer in Nietzsche's later thought, and Nietzsche explicitly recognizes this connection in one passage in the *Genealogy of Morals,* where he quotes from Schopenhauer. Schopenhauer is glorifying art as an escape from the domination of the will. "This is the painless state which Epicurus praised as the highest good and the state of the gods; we are during this moment freed from the vile pressure of the will, we celebrate the Sabbath of the will's hard labour, the wheel of Ixion stands still."[17]

All these quotations, with their wide implications, throw light on

[13] Cf. *Stories,* p. 21.
[14] *Stories,* p. 6.
[15] Not included in the English edition. German Musarion edition, xvi, p. 145. "Studies from the period of the 'Transvaluation,' 1882–88."
[16] 16, p. 166.
[17] 13, p. 132.

the significance of Friedemann's fate. The problem in Friedemann is in fact a variant on the Nietzsche-Schopenhauer conflict. As a typical decadent, Friedemann has tried to create a life in which his dominant instincts are suppressed; but however subtly he tries to escape, he cannot renounce the forces that are the springs of life itself.

In *The Dilettante* it is all the more clear that Mann fears, in a truly Nietzschean fashion, that a life eluding the realities of the will is meaningless and without values. Again we have the particular circumstances of Mann's own early life: the rich, north German business family in the old Gothic city, the same relationship between father and mother, incidents of his childhood that were to be repeated in *Buddenbrooks* and *Tonio Kröger*. The hero is once again separated from his companions by his talent and sensitivity. But he is incapable of action, he is unable to give his energies to any particular task. Able to live without working on what he inherits from his father, he settles down in Munich to a life spent in the amiable enjoyment of literature and the arts. Suffering a growing sense of disillusionment here, he cannot disguise a feeling of doubt and insecurity. He makes no contacts, either bourgeois or Bohemian, and he holds back, unpleasantly aware that he cannot justify himself, "that he cannot make clear even to a drunken painter exactly who and what he is."[18]

The psychology is intimately personal to Mann. We feel he is expressing a fear of his own possible fate. But the conflict is also Nietzschean. The dilettante lacks the will to work and accomplishment; in the abstract sense the will to power. This is the reason for his collapse. Nietzsche says: "Life itself, to my mind, is nothing more nor less than the instinct of growth, of permanence, of accumulating forces, of power; where the will to power is lacking, degeneration sets in."[19] The capacity for achievement is an essential quality in man. "It is our *feeling of nobility* which forbids us from being simply *enjoyers* of existence—this feeling rouses itself against hedonism—we wish to *achieve something against it.*"[20]

The dilettante has nothing of his own to present against life. Consequently when, like Johannes Friedemann, he falls in love, a helpless sense of inadequacy prevents him from trying to achieve happiness; he retires in confusion before the glorious self-assurance of his rival. He gives up hope, but does not end dramatically like Friedemann; he feels he will go on filling up his days somehow, although

---

[18] *Stories*, p. 39.
[19] 16, p. 131.
[20] Not included in the English edition. German Musarion edition, xiv, p. 235. "From the period of the 'Transvaluation,' 1883–88."

he is conscious of an inevitable process of dissolution working in him.

Mann's reliance on Nietzschean psychology is seen also in the short sketch *Tobias Mindernickel* that appeared with the other stories in the 1898 collection. The will to power is again the dominant motivating force. Mindernickel is a weak, submissive man whose appearance seems to betray a shrinking humility before the world. Whenever he leaves his room, the boys in the neighborhood ridicule him and throw stones. On one occasion, however, when one of the boys mocking him falls and cuts his head, Mindernickel seems to show a more favorable side of his nature. He comforts the boy and encourages him. But this opportunity to return good for evil is not born of Christian charity. It is taken because it offers Mindernickel the chance of releasing his need for power—a power he can exercise in pity. This becomes clear when he shortly buys a dog from which he can demand complete devotion and submission. When the dog resists him and will no longer submit to Mindernickel's demand for love and obedience, his urge for authority becomes an insane rage, and in a fury he wounds the animal to keep it completely at his mercy. The suspect origin of gentleness and pity is an essential feature of Nietzsche's "unmasking psychology." One passage in *Human, All-Too-Human* expresses precisely the theme of this story.

Pity...is in so far a consolation for the weak and suffering in that the latter recognize therein they *possess still one power*, in spite of their weakness, *the power of giving pain*. The unfortunate derives a sort of pleasure from this feeling of superiority of which the exhibition of pain makes him conscious; his imagination is exalted; he is still powerful enough to give the world pain.[21]

One other story, *Disillusionment*, that appeared in Mann's first collection of short stories provides interesting supporting evidence of his concern with Nietzsche. The central character here expresses a reaction to the world very closely related to that of Friedemann and the "Dilettante." His life too is removed from immediately felt experiences and emotions. He is cut off and alone. This time, however, he does not share any of the outward circumstances of Mann's life. Instead, what we learn of his family background recalls Nietzsche's childhood. He comes, as he tells us, from a clergyman's family in central Germany, and has been brought up in an atmosphere of "pulpit rhetoric and large words for good and evil." At his home there was a punctilious cleanliness, and the "pathetic optimism of the scholarly atmosphere" prevailed.[22]

---

[21] 6, p. 69.
[22] *Stories*, p. 24.

The fact that the scene is set in Venice, which is apparently other-wise irrelevant, also suggests a relation to Nietzsche. The importance of this city in Nietzsche's life—it was the place, he said, where he felt he could do his best work, and also where his closest friend Peter Gast resided—seems to have led Mann to associate it with the philosopher. With deliberate reference to Nietzsche, it becomes the scene for *Death in Venice.*

The narrator meets a stranger on the steps of San Marco who tells him of the disillusionment he has suffered in all his experiences of life. Nothing that he has felt corresponds to what he had hoped from it. Fine phrases and poetic enthusiasm arouse expectations of a life that is filled with rich emotions—feelings of perfect happiness or fear-ful horror. Instead, he is disappointed by all that he had dreamed of; he is bound by the limitations of reality. He quotes from Goethe's *Werther:* "What is man ... man, the glorious half-god? Do not his powers fail him just where he needs them most?"[23] Poets tell us that words are poor things when we try to express the richness and color of life. But no, he had found the poverty and limitations of life in-tolerable in comparison with the wealth of poetic expression.

Zarathustra in his attacks on the poets declares: "The poets lie too much. ... Ah, there are so many things betwixt heaven and earth of which the poets have only dreamed!"[24]

It is at first surprising that Mann should seem to associate this mood of youthful romantic pessimism with Nietzsche. It is a mood that seems closer, as the quotation implies, to the emotions of Goethe's youth. But Mann's aproach to Nietzsche is always a personal one: it is significant that what he should already see in Nietzsche is a man struggling with the Werther-like nihilism of his own thought. This interpretation has remained the key to Mann's sympathetic under-standing of Nietzsche's life. He is not concerned with what Nietzsche stated or argued, but with the psychological origins of Nietzsche's work. He saw in this work a reflection of emotions and sentiments intimately akin to his own.

Although the evidence of Nietzschean influence appears frequently in the short stories, the major novel *Buddenbrooks,* which Mann had already started and on which he was at work during the following years, gave little scope for a further interpretation of the philosopher. The subject matter for the novel lay at hand in the history of Mann's

---

[23] *Ibid.,* p. 26.
[24] 11, p. 153.

own family. His task was that of an artist; he had to work out the treatment of this vast theme.

The influence of his Nietzsche studies, however, may be seen in the consistency of values that helps to give the novel its unity. These were values already found in the early Novellen, judgments based in terms of health and sickness, weakness and strength. The development in Thomas Buddenbrook's generation of a more sensitive temperament and a deeper capacity of feeling brings at the same time a loss of vitality and self-confidence, an inner sense of meaninglessness, which contrasts with the healthy assurance of the earlier generations. The cultural and moral standards of the patriarchal middle class are not discussed in themselves; Mann is not concerned with making a judgment or criticism of them. Rather, the traditional bourgeois life is the accepted condition imposed on his characters, a particular form that the very nature of life itself has assumed. In this world the healthy have the will to survive, the urge to take part in the battle that the world of commerce demands. As Thomas Buddenbrook recognizes, "Life was harsh: And business, with its ruthless unsentimentality, was an epitome of life."[25] At the same time their conscience is easy because they are playing an acceptable role in the community's life, automatically, without any sense of problem, accepting the limits communal interest has imposed on the instinctive urge for dominance and power.

Mann accepts in effect Nietzsche's disclosure of ruthless, egoistic self-assertion as the basic factor of human nature, as of all organic life.

Life itself is *essentially* appropriation, injury, conquest of the strange and weak, suppression, severity, obtrusion of its own forms, incorporation, and at the least, putting it mildest, exploitation....

"Exploitation" does not belong to a depraved, or imperfect and primitive society; it belongs to the *nature* of the living being as a primary organic function; it is a consequence of the intrinsic Will to Power, which is precisely the Will to Life. Granting that as a theory this is a novelty—as a reality it is the *fundamental fact* of all history: let us be so far honest towards ourselves![26]

Near the end of the novel, after the account of Hanno's melancholy day at school, Mann claims that those who are fit for life, "strong and capable for life as it is," find the arbitrariness and misery of the school's workings quite acceptable and natural.[27] The sons of the two branches of the Hagenström family are perfectly at home. Two of

[25] *Buddenbrooks*, p. 386. Copyright 1924 by Alfred A. Knopf, Inc.
[26] 12, p. 226.
[27] *Buddenbrooks*, p. 585.

them join happily in the rowdiness and cheating and bullying; the other two, like Tonio Kröger's friend Hans Hansen, prove excellent students, admired by the teachers for their hard work and enterprise. Hanno, who is uncomprehendingly aware that something is wrong, intuitively foresees that school is only the pattern in miniature of life outside, a life in which there is no part for him to play. What can become of him? He can hardly become a musician, yet there is nothing else he would like to do or be. In despair he cries out to his friend Kai: "I'd like to sleep and never wake up. I'd like to die!"[28] And he does die; the typhoid fever that attacks him seems just a name given to death itself, which, as if certain of its victim, comes undisguised.

In contrast, his grandfather Consul Johann Buddenbrook the second and his grandmother Betsy had clung to life with an indomitable tenacity. Johann survived many accidents in his youth. On one occasion he nearly drowned. There is no question of heroism in his rescue; someone grasps him by the hair as he comes up for the third time, and Johann relentlessly seizes his arm and will not let go, although the rescuer, fearing he will be dragged in himself, struggles to break away and even bites Johann's hand.

Johann Buddenbrook and his father, though of different generations reflecting different customs and different concepts of morality and taste, both have an instinctive acceptance for the conditions under which they experience life as something self-evident. Neither the one's amiable eighteenth-century skepticism nor the voluble piety of the other affects his alert and vigorous sense for business and the reality of power. Both accept as a matter of course the way the world is made, and both have an instinctive sense of appropriateness that they are born to command. Although these unimaginative businessmen are in no sense Nietzschean heroes, it is clear they possess a sense of rightful authority that is lacking in the next generation and that Nietzsche demanded of his great men. In the discussion "What is noble?" (in *Beyond Good and Evil*) Nietzsche emphasizes that the great man characteristically "accepts the fact of his egoism without question; also without consciousness of harshness, constraint, or arbitrariness therein, but rather as something that may have its basis in the primary law of things."[29]

Of Consul Buddenbrook's three children, only Thomas seems the strong and determined protagonist of his family's position. But as the story unfolds, we learn of the discipline and courage Thomas required

[28] *Ibid.*, p. 592.
[29] 12, p. 240.

of himself in order to carry on his work. Still only in his thirties, he finds that his early vitality has begun to ebb away. He feels tired and old and uncertain of himself. In a mood of despondency he recalls the imaginative energy of his youth and the character of his ambitions.

To work at his play, to play at his work, to bend an ambition that was half-earnest, half-whimsical, toward the accomplishment of aims that even to himself possessed but a symbolic value—for such blithe scepticism and such an enlightened spirit of compromise, a great deal of vitality is necessary, as well as a sense of humour.[30]

Many elements had shown the equivocal nature of his business career. His culture, his pleasure in quoting from Goethe, his personal elegance, his inclination toward the aristocratic and the superfine, all reveal a decided change from the simple, straightforward lives of his predecessors. There is also his marriage with the romantic, music-loving Gerda. When he married, he had felt strong and free enough to show the world his taste in choosing a wife outside the narrow bourgeois circle. But the tact and restraint of feeling this marriage imposes are only another demand he makes on himself. When Thomas becomes senator his work calls on all his capacities—his flexibility and foresight and power to charm—but it is then he finds he is losing his elasticity and growing tired. Thomas had imagined himself a simple, practical man. Now he realizes this had been an ambition consciously striven for, a task he had set himself. He had been playing out a part, a role that life imposed on him. But behind all that he had accomplished is revealed the inner emptiness of the actor. Thomas had been withdrawn from all true emotion or genuine experience. He had lost all secure relationship to life.

In a passage in *Zarathustra*, Nietzsche laments the triumph of actors and mountebanks who gain acclamation and reward for their imitations of greatness. At the same time, the really great man is forced to flee from the market place into his solitude. Only there will he be free to develop, only there can he find himself.

Where solitude endeth, there beginneth the market-place; and where the market-place beginneth, there beginneth also the noise of the great actors, and the buzzing of poisonous flies.

In the world even the best things are worthless without those who represent them; those representers, the people call great men.

Little do people understand what is great—that is to say, the creating agency. But they have a taste for all representers and actors of great things.[31]

---

[30] *Buddenbrooks*, p. 493.
[31] 11, p. 57.

Because he has devoted himself to it Thomas Buddenbrook seems to lead the family to its greatest triumph, and he is acclaimed throughout the town. But success cannot disguise the fact that he does not really fit into the world of commerce, nor does he have the particular lack of conscience that, as Nietzsche insists, the true born actor requires. "Spirit, hath the actor, but little conscience of the spirit. He believeth always in that wherewith he maketh believe most strongly— in *himself.*"[32] Thomas' faith in himself dissolves. He recognizes the division within himself, and from this division occurs the early breakdown of his powers. Although there is a certain rigidity and a lack of psychological realism in this mechanistic calculation of a man wearing himself out through the expenditure of his nervous energy, it is for that very reason a clear indication of Mann's thought, as the logical plan of his work.

The control and self-discipline of Thomas' life are the means that enable him to resist the urge to despair that threatens him from within. His family pride and his intellectual and cultural pretensions help him to carry on his life. Only in the face of his imminent death and the disintegration of his family ambitions does he turn to Schopenhauer to find support from outside. Here he finds revenge at last for the suffering life has brought.

He was filled with a great, surpassing satisfaction. It soothed him to see how a master-mind could lay hold on this strong, cruel, mocking thing called life and enforce it and condemn it. His was the gratification of the sufferer who has always had a bad conscience about his sufferings and concealed them from the gaze of a harsh, unsympathetic world, until suddenly, from the hand of an authority, he receives, as it were, justification and licence for his suffering—justification before the world, this best of all possible worlds which the master-mind scornfully demonstrates to be the worst of all possible ones![33]

The chapter on "Death and its relation to the indestructibility of our true nature" most absorbs Thomas. Schopenhauer is attempting to show that the individual should not fear death, which destroys only the personal in him, whereas the essence of man which is his will lives on in others. This lesson arouses in Thomas a curious reaction. He finds satisfaction in knowing that life will continue in those who are stronger than he. It is not the unhappy Hanno who will be his heir, but all those who are able to rejoice in life as it is, all those who say "I," and—above all—those who say it with joy and confidence. He has not hated life—only himself, because he can no longer endure life.

[32] 11, p. 58.
[33] *Buddenbrooks,* p. 524.

"Have I ever hated life—pure, strong, relentless life? Folly and mis-conception! I have but hated myself, because I could not bear it."[34]

In this reaction we feel the reflection, not of Schopenhauer, but of Nietzsche, who had "overcome Schopenhauer," and who sought to conquer the decadence within him. Whereas for Schopenhauer victory lay in the ascetic denial of the will—the achieving of a condition where we are free from its power—it is Nietzsche who sees precisely in the will the force of life that is creative and affirmative.

Thomas Buddenbrook has asserted his will to achievement in the face of a life of suffering, and even in his collapse he affirms the need for this assertion. This "heroism from weakness" is characteristic of Mann's ideal. The need to find in the face of destructive self-knowledge a basis for meaningful action remains the problem of Mann's work. It is this problem that brings him back constantly to Nietzsche, and it is for this reason that the relationship with Nietzsche remains a central factor in the development of Mann's thought.

---

[34] *Ibid.*, p. 527.

# III. TONIO KRÖGER

IT IS EASY to imagine the growth of self-confidence Thomas Mann must have felt after the success of *Buddenbrooks*. His future was now settled. In the *Sketch of My Life,* Mann describes the enthusiasm with which his novel was received. It brought him fame and wealth. His picture appeared in the papers, the world greeted him with congratulations and praise. He began to feel confident and justified. The facts of his career were given in the German equivalent of *Who's Who*. As a successful writer he too was now satisfactorily enrolled in this compilation of bourgeois achievement. He was no longer embarrassed to discuss the circumstances of his daily life, to explain the nature of his guilty resistance to the demands of regularity made on him by the world. In the early autobiographical essay of 1907 "In the Mirror,"[1] Mann describes with pleasant irony the years of idleness in Italy, where he had passed the days in scribbling and in reading belles-lettres, a "pastime which at the most might serve a decent man as relaxation for his hours of leisure." These lost years were now accounted for, and the guardians and teachers of his youth who had so justifiably foreseen his failure had to accept the fact that he had not met his expected fate at all. Mann's amiably satirical tone scarcely disguises his pride in his achievement. There is plenty of other evidence of his newly found confidence. Heinrich Mann describes it in his recently published memoirs:

Once this novel had appeared with its attendant success, I never saw him suffering from life again. Or rather he was now strong enough to deal with it. The last capable man of the family was by no means gone. My brother showed throughout the constancy of our father, as well as the ambition which had been his virtue.[2]

The growth of confidence is reflected in the six Novellen that appeared in 1903 under the collective title *Tristan*. In the two principal stories of this collection, *Tonio Kröger* and *Tristan* itself, Mann deals for the first time specifically with the problem of the creative artist. Although the hero is still an isolated figure, he is no longer, as he was in the earlier stories, merely an outcast, unable to find a place in society; he is also a writer, a man who has for good or bad chosen his profession.

[1] Reprinted in *Rede und Antwort* (Berlin, 1922), a collection of early essays that has not been translated.
[2] Heinrich Mann, *Ein Zeitalter wird besichtigt* (Berlin, 1947). These memoirs have not been translated.

Of the collection, *Tonio Kröger* is the most valuable story for an understanding of Mann's development. Here he discusses the value and motivation of his work as an artist. From the standpoint of achievement—Kröger too has already produced a work of acknowledged merit—Mann can afford ruthlessly to analyze the suspect nature of his own creative work and its dubious origins. Through this harsh self-analysis he comes to understand where his real task as an artist lies.

*Tonio Kröger* is the most personal of all Mann's writings. Mann himself said, as late as 1930, that of all he had written this story remained the dearest to his heart.[3] Mann calls it "my most intimate work" and tells us of a student in Göttingen with a thin, nervous face who, after Mann had read the story aloud in a café there, declared: " 'I hope you know, don't you, it is not *Buddenbrooks* which is your most intimate work—it is *Tonio Kröger!*' I said I knew it."[4]

At the same time it is in *Tonio Kröger* that Mann provides the first clear and consistent evidence of his deeply felt relationship with Nietzsche. Where in the earlier work Nietzsche's influence on his manner of thought could only be suggested and its significance guessed at, the confession of the artist is made in terms that are constantly reminiscent of Nietzsche, thereby emphasizing the intimate and essential connection between Nietzsche's fate and that of Mann's hero, so that Kröger's life can best be interpreted through an appreciation of Mann's relation to the philosopher's work.

The main theme of the tale was conceived while Mann was working on *Buddenbrooks* in Munich; its origins were in an excursion he made to Denmark via Lübeck and his impressions of a visit to Aalsgard am Sund near Helsingör. He wrote the story very slowly, and particularly the middle section—the conversation with Lisabeta—cost months of work.[5] Although begun so early, the tale did not appear in print until three years later. Like *Buddenbrooks, Tonio Kröger* was soon recognized and acclaimed.

The appeal of *Tonio Kröger* lies largely in the mood of youthful lyrical yearning and aspiration, passionately felt in the boy's helpless love for Hans Hansen and Ingeborg Holm, and still carried over into the abstractions of Tonio's conversation with Lisabeta. The short episodes of his youth, filled with poetic sympathy, are provided with significant experiences that can be transferred as symbols into the later discussions of Kröger's character and work. Phrases and combi-

---

[3] *Sketch of My Life*, p. 29.
[4] *Observations*, p. 60.
[5] *Sketch of My Life*, p. 29.

nations of themes that recall the mood and spirit of the early experiences are interwoven into Kröger's theoretical arguments. Particular experiences reappear in a new light, with a symbolic importance they would not possess in themselves, just as a musical theme or short phrase may take on a new significance when it is presented in a different and elevated context. These lingusitic "motifs" convey to the discussion in the middle section a unity of mood and at the same time a sense of personally lived experience. For in this conversation Kröger seems to relive his own life, and comes to understand what has been happening to him. Thus a new meaning is given the episodes already past, as well as an interpretation for the incidents to come. What might be a discursive and impersonal essay on the conflict of nature versus mind, life versus art, becomes a living experience imbued with profound feeling and sensibility.[6]

In *Tonio Kröger* Mann has presented his own circumstances as man and artist more completely than in any of the earlier stories. In a sense he draws together the elements in those stories that only partly gave the circumstances of his own life. The family background, the long-established business now coming to an end, the mother from an exotic southern country, the early experiences of Mann's youth—all are included. In particular *Tonio Kröger* stands in close relation to *Buddenbrooks;* it is, in Mann's own words, "a prose ballad played on the same instrument as the large novel."[7] Tonio may be seen as Hanno Buddenbrook grown up; the circumstances of his life in Lübeck are the same. The disintegration of the family, which had served as the subject for two long volumes, is summarized in a few lines in *Tonio Kröger.* Here is the final stage in the collapse.

His father's mother, the head of the family, had died, and not long after his own father followed, the tall, thoughful, carefully dressed gentleman with the field-flower in his buttonhole. The great Kröger house, with all its stately tradition, came up for sale, and the firm was dissolved.[8]

There was some reason to consider Tonio's own existence and way of life as one of the signs of decay. But if Tonio is Hanno, he has also acquired from Hanno's friend Kai a vitality and toughness that Hanno lacked—a capacity to resist the world, to oppose something of his own against it. It is this quality that appears in Tonio when he is grown up, and that is essential for him if he is to become an artist. It is an

    [6] Cf. a discussion of the artistry in *Tonio Kröger* in *Introduction to the Novelle,* by Elizabeth Wilkinson (Oxford, 1944).
    [7] *Observations,* p. 60.
    [8] *Stories,* p. 98.

element indeed that seemed lacking in Tonio as a boy, but that is the key to his development in maturity.

The personal element in *Tonio Kröger* has disguised the extent to which his confession reveals Mann's dependence upon Nietzsche. In more recent essays Mann has made a point of indicating the connections between Nietzsche and his hero. In a short discussion of his early work in an essay on "Freud and the Future" (1936),[9] Mann says that the melancholy of the young writer had reference to the Hamlet-like in Nietzsche's nature, in which his own nature mirrored itself. Again, in an essay on "Nietzsche's Philosophy in the Light of Contemporary Events," Mann introduces this parallel between Hamlet's fate and Nietzsche's. In both essays he characterizes this fate in an expression he had already used in *Tonio Kröger*. Analyzing his feeling for Nietzsche, he says it is: "The tragic pity for an overloaded, overcharged soul which was only called to knowledge, not really born to it and, like Hamlet, was destroyed by it."[10] Tonio Kröger, in the course of his confession to Lisabeta, describes his own fate as a man of letters in exactly these terms. He says it was: "The case of Hamlet, the Dane, that typical literary man. He knew what it meant to be called to knowledge without being born to it."[11]

A passage in *The Birth of Tragedy* that reveals Nietzsche's own impression of Hamlet emphasizes the relevance of this association. He is illustrating the problems of the "Dionysian" man: "In this sense the Dionysian man may be said to resemble Hamlet: both have for once seen into the true nature of things,—they have *perceived* and they are loath to act. . . . Knowledge kills action, action requires the veil of illusion—it is this lesson which Hamlet teaches . . ."[12]

This common relationship to Hamlet indicates the nature of the connection between Kröger and Nietzsche. Kröger longs for a place in normal, straightforward, regular life, but he is doomed to isolation, to knowledge, and to solitude. He feels he is condemned to knowing; it is his fate to be impelled to estimate and understand the motives of men's actions and his own. Even as a fourteen-year-old boy, he feels himself so organized that he is consciously instructed by his experiences of life; he writes them down as it were inwardly; and he feels how difficult it is to see through the reasons for others' behavior, when

---

[9] *Essays of Three Decades*, p. 413.

[10] *Nietzsche's Philosophy in the Light of Contemporary Events* (Washington, 1947), p. 4. An address at the Library of Congress.

[11] *Stories*, p. 106.

[12] 1, pp. 61–62.

they live so simply and easily.[13] Their gaze is tranquil and imperturbable; they do not look into things until their eyes become complicated and sad. Kröger is condemned "to see through everything." It is his curse as well as his pride.

Nietzsche's fate too was that of a man for whom love was a necessity, who required friendship and understanding and yet was reduced to isolation and loneliness. In the essay on "Nietzsche's Philosophy in the Light of Contemporary Events," Mann puts into words the concept he had always held of Nietzsche's work as a tormented search for truth. He describes Neitzsche's life as a heroic journey into uncharted worlds of thought, taken with a courageous acceptance of suffering and self-torture. He sees him as a martyr driven on in the search for truth, whose task is to uncover disguises, to penetrate the pretenses in which man attempts to find consolation and support. Nietzsche is always most demanding on himself, refusing any solace. The truth is always to be found in what brings him pain, in the tortured denial of everything that might grant him security and ease. "The strength of a man's mind," Nietzsche writes in *Beyond Good and Evil*, "might be measured in the amount of truth it could endure—or to speak more plainly, by the extent to which it *required* truth attenuated, veiled, sweetened, damped, and falsified."[14]

When Tonio leaves his home town, he goes to "large cities and in the south." He submits himself to the power of literature, the power of intellect and the word, which "lords it with a smile over the unconscious and inarticulate." This power sharpens his eyes:

It ... made him see through the large words which puff out the bosoms of mankind; it opened for him men's souls and his own, made him clairvoyant, showed him the inwardness of the world and the ultimate behind men's words and deeds. And all that he saw could be put in two words: the comedy and the tragedy of life.

And then, with knowledge, its torment and its arrogance, came solitude; because he could not endure the blithe and innocent with their darkened understanding, while they in turn were troubled by the sign on his brow.[15]

At first the practice of his art brings compensation for his isolation, the gulf of ironic sensibility, knowledge, and skepticism that separated him from his fellows. But as he finds his work becoming the whole meaning of his life—so that he does not work simply to live, but as one who is bent on doing nothing but work—there arises in him a growing abhorrence for the life to which he is inevitably committed.

---

[13] Cf. *Stories*, p. 91.
[14] 12, pp. 53–54.
[15] *Stories*, p. 99.

In the conversation with Lisabeta, Kröger laments his destiny and cries out in passion against the curse of knowledge and the torment of artistic creation.

"Well, now to come back to the 'knowledge.' Can't you imagine a man, born orthodox, mild-mannered, well-meaning, a bit sentimental, just simply over-stimulated by his psychological clairvoyance, and going to the dogs? Not to let the sadness of the world unman you; to read, mark, learn, and put to account even the most torturing things and to be of perpetual good cheer, in the sublime consciousness of moral superiority over the horrible invention of existence—yes, thank you! But despite all the joys of expression once in a while the thing gets on your nerves. *'Tout comprendre c'est tout pardonner.'* I don't know about that. There is something I call being sick of knowledge, Lisabeta; when it is enough for you to see through a thing in order to be sick to death of it, and not in the least in a forgiving mood. Such was the case of Hamlet the Dane, that typical literary man."[16]

The traces of Nietzsche are to be found throughout this speech. When Kröger laments that a man of good nature might feel himself over-stimulated and condemned simply by the force and clarity of his psychological insight, we recognize the same mood of disillusionment with knowledge so movingly expressed in Nietzsche. At the time of *Human, All-Too-Human*, Nietzsche writes, for example:

As a matter of fact a certain blind belief in the goodness of human nature, an innate aversion to the analysis of human actions, a kind of shamefacedness with respect to the nakedness of the soul may really be more desirable for the general well-being of a man than that quality, useful in isolated cases, of psychological sharp-sightedness; and perhaps the belief in goodness, in virtuous men and deeds, in an abundance of impersonal good-will in the world, has made men better inasmuch as it has made them less distrustful.[17]

A mistrust of knowledge is apparent throughout Nietzsche. Knowledge brings disgust and a sense of hopelessness. Already in the early essays *Thoughts Out of Season* and, in part, *The Birth of Tragedy* Nietzsche subordinates the urge to knowledge to the need for a fruitful culture. The value of history, for example, exists only as it is necessary for life, not as an idle escape into the garden of knowledge. Later— at the time of *Human, All-Too-Human*, where he requires the keenest sense of truth from his followers and seeks a "free spirit" exempt from all prejudgments—he recognizes, still with the same poignancy, that knowledge means suffering. He quotes a passage from Byron's *Manfred* (Act I, Scene I) that might be taken as a motto for the theme of *Tonio Kröger:*

---
[16] *Ibid.*, p. 106.
[17] 6, pp. 54–55.

Sorrow is knowledge: They who know the most
Must mourn the deepest o'er the fatal truth,
The Tree of Knowledge is not that of Life.[18]

One phrase that Kröger uses to Lisabeta, "disgust with knowledge" (in German, "Erkenntnisekel"), has a decidedly Nietzschean character. "Ekel" ("disgust"), is a word used constantly by Nietzsche. "Disgust with mankind was always my greatest danger," he writes in *Ecce Homo*.[19] This disgust arises from knowledge of the pettiness of man's motives, the misery of his ambitions and ideals. Knowledge for Nietzsche (and for Kröger) is psychology, knowledge of man's soul. Zarathustra, the prophet of a new man, gains victory over this aversion. He is "the man without disgust, the conqueror of his great disgust," because he has a vision of man free from his pitiable weaknesses.

Kröger goes on to say that a man must not allow himself to be overcome by the sadness of the world. He must become master of his suffering, "in the consciousness of moral superiority," still joyful in knowledge. This was Nietzsche's task: to be above suffering, to accept life with joyful affirmation in spite of all its sorrow. This is the importance of Nietzsche's concept of the "eternal return." A man must live as if he were to live thus eternally—and this is the most difficult of all tasks.

Kröger wonders that knowledge is said to bring relief. " 'Tout comprendre c'est tout pardonner' I don't know about that." Possibly Mann has in mind Nietzsche's revision of this dictum: "Tout comprendre c'est tout mépriser."

We no longer believe that truth remains truth when it is *unveiled*,—we have lived enough to understand this.... Today it seems to us good form not to strip everything naked, not to be present at all things, not to desire to "know" all. "Tout comprendre c'est tout mépriser"....

Oh these Greeks, they understood the art of *living!* For this it is necessary to halt bravely at the surface, at the fold, at the skin, to worship appearance, and to believe in forms, tones, words, and the whole *Olympus of appearance!* These Greeks were superficial from *profundity*....

*Greeks?* Worshippers of form, of tones, of words? Precisely on that account— *artists?*[20]

Kröger's cry against knowledge continues:

"Then another and no less charming side of the thing, of course, is your ennui, your indifferent and ironic attitude towards truth. It is a fact that there is

[18] 6, p. 112.
[19] 17, p. 26.
[20] 8, p. 82.

no society in the world so dumb and hopeless as a circle of literary people who are hounded to death as it is. All knowledge is old and tedious to them."[21]

In the German the expression used—"Müdigkeit der Wahrheit gegenüber" ("weariness toward the truth")—again recalls Nietzschean phraseology. The enemy Zarathustra struggles bitterly to overcome is the "great weariness." "No longer willing, and no longer valuing, and no longer creating! Ah, that that great debility may ever be far from me."[22] Zarathustra comes as a strong wind, "a fresh, blustering wind," to destroy all who are "tired on the journey" and all who are "prophets of the great weariness."[23]

Knowledge brings exhaustion and disgust. But Kröger cannot find compensation for this torment in his art. His experience had been at first that the pleasures of expression and the composition of his work had kept him alert and of good cheer, when knowledge would otherwise have made him melancholy. In the conversation with Lisabeta he has become doubtful of the very nature of his work. Kröger's art springs from the very same qualities that prevent his taking a happy part in normal life. His development as an artist grows at the expense of his life as a human being. His loneliness arises from a deep sense of failure as a man. He poignantly expresses his fear that he is outside life, condemned to observe when others are living:

"To see things clear, if even through your tears, to recognize, notice, observe—and have to put it all down with a smile, at the very moment when hands are clinging, and lips meeting, and the human gaze is blinded with feeling. . . ."[24]

Thus he is led to question the dubious nature of an artist whose work does not flow from a full heart but is the result of disciplined study and fastidious care. He expresses this doubt with an exaggeration and irony that, like his occasional understatement, really conceals deep feeling.

At the bottom of his soul, Kröger says, he feels all the scorn and suspicion of the artist gentry—translated into intellectual terms—that his upright forebears on the Baltic felt for any juggler or mountebank. The banker who has a gift for writing stories is also a criminal. Kröger cannot escape the suspicion that the source and essence of his being an artist are what brought him to prison. A banker who is irreproachably respectable and yet writes—such a man does not exist.

[21] *Stories*, p. 107.
[22] 11, p. 101.
[23] 11, p. 251.
[24] *Stories*, pp. 106–107.

The enthusiast and the beginner imagine the artist to be a man of warm emotions and to have a tender heart. Feeling, Kröger argues, is always banal and futile. If an artist too deeply feels what he has to say, if his heart is too much in it, he will likely succeed only in becoming pathetic and sentimental. The artist must be unhuman, extra-human, and stand in a strange aloof relationship to humanity. The very gifts of style, form, and expression can arise only from this cool and fastidious attitude. Kröger has nothing but scorn for the dilettante or for the enthusiast roused to excitement by the effect of a work of art. A number of examples establish this attitude: the innocent enthusiasm of Kröger's admirers; the lieutenant with the urge to write verses, whose poem—something about love and music—Kröger finds "as deeply felt as it is inept." Then there is the simplicity of the enthusiasm of Kröger's fellow passenger on the trip to Denmark—a young man who "probably writes good, homely, business man's verses," and who shows a somewhat ingenuous enthusiasm for the glory and magnitude of nature. Unfortunately, after a heavy meal of lobster omelet, he is not feeling too well. " 'Lord!' he said in a hollow, quavering voice, when he saw Tonio Kröger. 'Look at the uproar of the elements, sir!' But he could say no more—he was obliged to turn hastily away."[25]

These passages are written with an amusing extravagance, but nevertheless they are intended seriously. " 'You laugh, Lisabeta, but yet I am only half joking.' "

What does it mean in fact to be an artist? he asks Lisabeta.

"Nothing shows up the general human dislike of thinking, and man's innate craving to be comfortable, better than his attitude to this question. When these worthy people are affected by a work they say humbly that that sort of thing is a 'gift.' And because in their innocence they assume that beautiful and uplifting results must have beautiful and uplifting causes, they never dream that the 'gift' in question is a very dubious affair and rests upon extremely sinister foundations."[26]

Kröger's judgment of the artist seems to arise out of his own most personal problems and to originate in Mann's own experience. At the same time, there is evidence of a close and deliberate parallel with Nietzschean thought.

In his early work Nietzsche, following Schopenhauer, had conceived of the artist as the great man, as hero and genius. But very soon the sincerity of the artist is questioned. His morality is weak exactly where Nietzsche demands strength: in his sense of truth—truth in the expres-

[25] *Ibid.*, p. 121.
[26] *Ibid.*, pp. 104–105.

sion of the realities his understanding mind perceives. Nietzsche wrote in his *Human, All-Too-Human:* "The artist . . . will on no account let himself be deprived of brilliant and profound interpretations of life . . . He will not renounce the *most effective* suppositions for his art, . . . The sense of the symbolical, the overvaluation of personality, the belief that genius is something miraculous . . . He considers, therefore, the continuance of his art of creation as more important than the scientific devotion to truth."[27] The idea of genius itself in the artist is questioned in a manner that recalls Kröger's contempt for the layman's comfortable suggestion that it is a "gift." These worthy persons speak of the spark of genius because then they need feel no envy of such a man outside their circumscribed world. As Nietzsche says, "To call anyone 'divine' is as much as saying: 'here we have no occasion for rivalry.' "[28] At the same time, it is to the artist's interest to perpetuate the idea of a divine gift.

It is to the interest of the artist that there should be a belief in sudden suggestions, so-called inspirations; as if the idea of a work of art, of poetry, the fundamental thought of a philosophy shone down from heaven like a ray of grace. In reality the imagination of the good artist or thinker constantly produces good, mediocre, and bad, but his *judgment,* most clear and practised, rejects and chooses and joins together . . .[29]

Nietzsche's rejection of the artist is closely associated with his split with Wagner. Nietzsche's relationship with the composer—his early love, his gradual resistance to the work and final repudiation of it— is one of the central themes in Nietzsche's life. When Nietzsche refers to art or the artist, it is nearly always clear that he has Wagner in mind.[30] Wagner is the artist par excellence. In *The Case of Wagner* Nietzsche attempts to examine the importance to his own work of his experiences with Wagner. In the preface he summarily rejects the idea of playing off another artist against Wagner. Wagner is the representative, almost symbolical, figure for modern art as such, who speaks its most deeply personal language:

And what better guide, or more thoroughly efficient revealer of the soul, could be found for the labyrinth of the modern spirit than Wagner? Through Wagner modernity speaks her most intimate language; it conceals neither its good nor its

---

[27] 6, p. 154.
[28] 6, p. 166.
[29] 6, p. 159. This is certainly the method of work of Mann's artists. Cf. especially Aschenbach in *Death in Venice.*
[30] Thomas Mann himself asserts this in the *Observations:* "Everywhere in these writings [i.e., Nietzsche's] when he speaks of artists and art, there the name Wagner should be unquestionably introduced, whether it is missing in the text or not" (p. 40).

evil; it has thrown off all shame ... I should understand a philosopher who said: "Wagner is modernity in concentrated form." There is no help for it, we must first be Wagnerites.[31]

For Thomas Mann also the "artist" meant essentially Wagner. All his life Mann has remained consistently loyal to his love for Wagner, and is anxious to find that Nietzsche too could never actually deny the power of his own love. Both in the *Observations*[32] and in the essay on "Nietzsche's Philosophy in the Light of Contemporary Events,"[33] Mann recalls with pleasure the passage in *Ecce Homo* where at this late date Nietzsche still refers to the "holy hour" of Wagner's death, and where he writes:

But to this day I am still seeking for a work which would be a match to *Tristan* in dangerous fascination, and possesses the same gruesome and dulcet quality of infinity; I seek among all the arts in vain.[34]

As I have already mentioned, Mann's love for Wagner is always conditioned by his knowledge and acceptance of Nietzsche's later criticism. Unlike Nietzsche, Mann was never deceived by the nature of Wagner's work. From the beginning, Mann is skeptical of the artist as such, conscious of the evidence of decadence that Wagner's work provides in the light of Nietzsche's criticism.

It is not surprising then that Kröger's analysis of the artist leads with a certain inevitability to Wagner's *Tristan und Isolde*.

"Take the most miraculous case of all, take the most typical and therefore the most powerful of artists, take such a morbid and profoundly equivocal work as *Tristan and Isolde*, and look at the effect it has on a healthy young man of thoroughly normal feelings."[35]

In this connection it is interesting to note the use Mann makes of the word "effect" ("Wirkung") in this passage. The artist is concerned with the effect he makes on his audience, not in presenting the truth. "To make the greatest possible effect, that is the artist's aim," Nietzsche says contemptuously in the chapter "Concerning the soul of artists and authors" in *Human, All-Too-Human*.[36] The essence of the writer's

---

[31] 8, p. xxxi.

[32] P. 41.

[33] P. 10.

[34] 17, pp. 43–44. For further evidence that Nietzche's love for Wagner remained in spite of all the violence of his criticism, compare his letter to his sister as late as February 22, 1887. He writes of *Parsifal*, which he has just seen: "I felt so elevated by this work, so transported, that I can think of it only with rapture" (*Gesammelte Briefe*, vol. 5, part 2, pp. 710–711).

[35] *Stories*, p. 105.

[36] 6, p. 153.

craft is the working out of a good point and effect. "Eine Pointe und Wirkung ausarbeiten" is a phrase repeated throughout *Tonio Kröger*. Kröger reports his friend Adalbert the novelist using the expression:

" 'God damn the spring!' says he in the aggressive way he has. 'It is and always has been the most ghastly time of the year. Can you get hold of a single sensible idea, Kröger? Can you sit still and work out even the smallest [point and] effect, when your blood tickles till it's positively indecent and you are teased by a whole host of irrelevant sensations that when you look at them turn out to be unworkable trash!' "[37]

The phrase is used again when Kröger visits his old home, now a public library, and takes a book off the shelves. Hs is familiar with the work, and reads it in the manner of a professional studying a fellow crafts-man. "He followed the black lines of print, the paragraphs, the flow of words that flowed with so much art, mounting in the ardour of crea-tion to a certain [point and] effect and then as artfully breaking off. . . ."[38] Again, when, to confirm his identity to the suspicious hotel manager and policeman, he hands over the manuscript of a story he is writing, he is pleased to find they hit upon a satisfactory passage, "a little effect he had worked out to a perfection."[39] This elaboration of an effect rounded off and artistically controlled has no relation to true sincerity of feeling. That is the significant fact. And it is hardly chance that the very word "effect" that is used with respect to Wagner's *Tristan und Isolde* is also applied to the activities of François Knaak the dancing master. When poor Tonio dances the woman's part in the quadrille, the audience is delighted by Knaak's reactions. Like an actor he makes the most of the episode, and the audience finds it as amusing as a play. "But Herr Heinzelmann at the piano sat and waited, with a dry, business-like air, for a sign to go on; he was hard-ened against Herr Knaak's effects."[40]

In another place, discussing the artist, Kröger brings in a parallel with the actor:

"I once knew an actor, a man of genius, who had to struggle with a morbid self-consciousness and instability. When he had no rôle to play, nothing to represent, this man, consummate artist but impoverished human being, was overcome by an exaggerated consciousness of his ego. A genuine artist—not one who has taken up art as a profession like another, but artist foreordained and damned—you can pick

---

[37] *Stories*, p. 102.
[38] *Ibid.*, p. 116. Slight alterations have been made in the text of the published translation here as well as in the one quoted directly above so that the phrase "Pointe und Wirkung" in German may be translated by one consistent English phrase.
[39] Cf. *ibid.*, p. 118.
[40] *Ibid.*, p. 96.

out, without boasting very sharp perceptions, out of a group of men. The sense of being set apart and not belonging, of being known and observed, something both regal and incongruous shows in his face."[41]

Kröger finds the public admire him, write him letters of praise and gratitude; but when he reads these letters, he blushes to feel what they would think if they saw behind the scenes and realized that a "properly constituted, healthy, decent man never writes, acts or composes." In the German, significantly, the word "mimt" is used for "acts." The miming of the actor is placed on a level with the art of the composer or the author.

It is at the basis of Nietzsche's repudiation of the artist that he sees him as an actor and pretender. The artist is not a man of deep and honest feelings, but like an actor he aims at a pretense of emotions that will be effective on the audience.

At the time of *Zarathustra*, Nietzsche wrote: "Everything I had said about Wagner was false. I felt it already in 1876: 'everything in him is ungenuine; all that is genuine is concealed or decorated. He is an actor in every good and bad sense of the word!' "[42] Again, in *The Case of Wagner:*

Wagner—*the rise of the actor in music* . . . his art develops itself more and more as a talent for lying.[43]

Wagner . . . an incomparable *histrio*, the greatest mime, the most astounding theatrical genius. . . .[44]

Indeed, during the period of *Human, All-Too-Human*, a whole section on "Art and authorship" had already been a variation of this theme. "The Muses as Liars. 'We know how to tell many lies,' so sang the Muses once. . . . The conception of the artist as deceiver, once grasped, leads to important discoveries."[45]

An aphorism in the fifth section of *Joyful Wisdom*, "The problem of the actor," most clearly summarizes what Nietzsche means by the artist as actor. The passage reveals the closeness of Nietzsche's concept of the artist with this aspect of Kröger's argument:

The problem of the actor has disquieted me the longest; I am uncertain . . . whether one could not get at the dangerous conception of "artist" . . . from this point of view. Falsity with a good conscience; delight in dissimulation breaking forth as

---

[41] *Ibid.*, p. 104.
[42] This material was not included in the English edition. German Musarion edition, xiv, p. 335. "Material for the later prefaces, 1885–1888."
[43] 8, pp. 32–33.
[44] 8, p. 23.
[45] 7, p. 101.

power; ... the inner longing to play a rôle, to assume a mask, to put on an *appearance;* a surplus of capacity for adaptions of every kind . . .; all that perhaps does not pertain *solely* to the actor in himself?"[46]

Hence Nietzsche finds an explanation for the problem he had already found difficult at the time of his admiration for Wagner in the essay in *Thoughts Out of Season.* How did Wagner succeed equally in such strangely contradictory works as *Tristan* and *Die Meistersinger?*[47] It is the capacity for adaptation to the subject matter, for pretense, something that further on in the same aphorism in *Joyful Wisdom* Nietzsche describes as comparable to the "mimicry" of animals—"the embodied and incarnated art of eternally playing the game of hide and seek."[48]

Kröger is aware of the equivocal nature of the artist's work and the falseness of the enthusiasm it arouses. Nevertheless he uses men's admiration for his genius to goad himself on, " 'taking it in deadly earnest and aping the airs of a great man.' "[49]

The artist is not only concerned with the simulation of emotions. His task is also to analyze and explain them. The writer must put everything into words, explain and thereby control it. Is this not also in effect a means of escaping from the experience of real feeling? What does the artist's work come to at the last? Kröger asks:

"[It is] a matter . . . of putting your emotions on ice and serving them up chilled! Honestly, don't you think there's a good deal of cool cheek in the prompt and superficial way a writer can get rid of his feelings by turning them into literature? If your heart is too full, if you are overpowered with the emotions of some sweet or exalted moment—nothing simpler! Go to the literary man, he will put it all straight for you instanter. He will analyse and formulate your affair, label it and express it and discuss it and polish it off. . . ."[50]

Much of our pleasure is to be found in the ordered and controlled. As Nietzsche says,

The sense of comfort in what is ordered and limited and comprehended, the satisfaction at repetition, these feelings give a sense of well-being to all organic creatures in face of the perils of their situation. . . . What is known does us good—the sight of something which we hope easily to *master.*

At the same time, the artist feels superiority and power in his capacity to organize his material and control his emotions.

---

[46] 10, p. 318.
[47] Cf. 4, p. 165.
[48] 10, p. 319.
[49] *Stories,* p. 103.
[50] *Ibid.,* p. 107.

The two aspects—the urge to authority and the capacity for pretense—are summarized in Nietzsche: *"Concerning the origin of art.—
The capacity for lying and concealing oneself developed over the longest period. Thereby a feeling of security and intellectual superiority in
the deceiver."*[51]

The artist becomes a lawgiver. "The reforming of the world in order
to bear life in it." A whole section of *The Will to Power* has been col-
lected under the heading: "The Will to Power as Art."[52]

The artist escapes from life, and yet seeks the illusion of superiority
and control over life itself. All the factors that make life difficult for
Tonio Kröger—his sensitivity, his lack of resistance to emotional
stimuli, the insight and taste that cut him off from his fellows, the
longing for love and understanding—can be absorbed in his work.
In this way the artist makes capital of his weaknesses.

In the *Dawn of Day*, Nietzsche writes:

To deal like an artist with one's weaknesses.—If we must positively have weaknesses and come in the end to look upon them as laws beyond ourselves, I wish
that everybody may be possessed of as much artistic capacity as will enable him
to set off his virtues by means of his weaknesses, and to make us, through his
weaknesses, desirous of acquiring his virtues; a power which great musicians have
possessed in quite an exceptional degree.[53]

The weaknesses become a virtue in the artist. They are indeed the
source of Kröger's work and the factors that attract us to him.

For Nietzsche it is a sign at the very heart of modern decadence
that the artist feels himself outside life, that a gap separates him from
an acceptable place in society. "How is *decadence* in *literature* characterized? By the fact that in it life no longer animates the whole."[54]
It is further, according to him, a consequence of this division that the
artist's work becomes a game in which formal perfection is substituted
for living emotion.

Artists take refuge in the beauty of form.[55]

A man is an artist to the extent to which he regards everything that inartistic
people call "form" as the actual substance, as the "principal" thing. With such
ideas a man certainly belongs to a world upside down; for henceforth substance
seems to him something merely formal,—his own life included.[56]

---

[51] Two passages not included in the English edition. German Musarion edition,
xvii, p. 304. "On art and artists, 1888."
[52] 15, p. 239.
[53] 9, p. 229.
[54] 8, p. 19.
[55] 15, p. 288.
[56] 15, p. 261.

The artist is sick and the product of a sick condition of humanity. This is the theme that the uncompleted *Will to Power* intended as an essential part of its comprehensive analysis of modern decadence. Art does not arise from a unity of life and feeling. It is hardly possible to be an artist and not be a sick man. "It is exceptional states that determine the artist—such states as are all intimately related and entwined with morbid symptoms, so that it would seem almost impossible to be an artist without being ill."[57] In *Ecce Homo,* discussing *Tristan und Isolde,* Nietzsche writes: "To become more healthy—this in a nature like Wagner's amounts to going backwards."[58] Wagner's work is created out of his sickness.

Tonio Kröger betrays the artist by showing him in the light in which Nietzsche had seen him. He refuses to accept everything that may be said on the other side, and rejects Lisabeta's reproaches when she says that he leaves out of consideration the purifying and healing influence of literature. Kröger claims he is aware of this point of view—the objections she raises are part of the things he has in mind—but he refuses to look at the question from this standpoint. Lisabeta suggests that literature, the product of knowledge and eloquence, may subdue the passions and become a guide to understanding and forgiveness. She speaks of the redeeming power of the word, and sees "the poet as the most highly developed of human beings, the poet as saint."[59] Kröger admits there is justification in what she says, especially considering her own Russian literature, but cannot see this as part of his own experience. The ennobling power of art? Possibly, but Kröger is a successful writer, Thomas Mann himself has achieved fame and recognition, and he can look back and ask this question coldly and with knowledge of accomplishment. The answer comes from Nietzsche; the artist who is so greatly honored is in fact a poor suffering creature, a victim and martyr. In *Beyond Good and Evil,* Nietzsche says:

Those great poets, for example, such as Byron, Musset, Poe, Leopardi, Kleist, Gogol (I do not venture to mention much greater names, but I have them in my mind), as they now appear, and were perhaps obliged to be; men of the moment, enthusiastic, sensuous, and childish; light-minded and impulsive in their trust and distrust; with souls in which usually some flaw has to be concealed; often taking revenge with their works for an internal defilement, often seeking forgetfulness in their soaring from a too true memory, often lost in the mud and almost

[57] 15, p. 254.
[58] 17, p. 44.
[59] *Stories,* p. 106.

in love with it, until they become like the Will o' the Wisps around the swamps, and *pretend to be* stars—the people then call them idealists,—often struggling with protracted disgust. . . . What *martyrs* these great artists are, and the so-called higher men in general, to him who has once found them out.[60]

Kröger has betrayed the artist and exploded the romantic illusions of genius. At the same time knowledge brings only disgust. A natural consequence of his arguments is that he comes directly to face the problem of nihilism—the denial of all values, the enemy with which Nietzsche had constantly to grapple.

"Nihilism is at our door: whence comes this most gruesome of all guests to us?"[61] This is the question at the beginning of *The Will to Power*. Kröger comes inevitably to this question, but cries out that he is not a nihilist. Lisabeta finds it difficult to believe. Kröger declares:

"I say I am not a nihilist, with respect, that is, to lively feeling. You see, the literary man does not understand that life may go on living, unashamed, even after it has been expressed and therewith finished. No matter how much it has been redeemed by becoming literature, it keeps on sinning—for all action is sin in the mind's eye—"[62]

It is his longing for life that will prove his salvation. This is the resolving theme throughout Kröger's experiences. His friend Adalbert the novelist retires into the neutral zone of the café when the spring arrives. There is too much feeling, too many "irrelevant sensations" that cannot be made use of. Kröger envies Adalbert his determination to escape from the triumphant natural force of spring, but cannot join him in his café. He had felt instinctively opposed to this, but only gradually comes to understand why. When the boy Tonio makes a fool of himself at the dancing class in Lübeck, he wonders why he came to be there; should he not be at home reading *Immensee?* But no, he rejects this.

But no, no, after all, his place was here, where he could feel near Inge, even although he stood lonely and aloof, seeking to distinguish the warm notes of her voice amid the buzzing, clattering, and laughter within.[63]

And yet! He stood there aloof and alone, staring hopelessly at a drawn blind and making, in his distraction, as though he could look out. But yet he was happy. For he lived. His heart was full; hotly and sadly it beat for thee, Ingeborg Holm . . .[64]

---

[60] 12, pp. 245–246.
[61] 14, p. 5.
[62] *Stories*, p. 107.
[63] *Ibid.*, p. 96.
[64] *Ibid.*, p. 97.

Through the years of his work, "in large cities and in the south," where he promised himself a luxuriant ripening of his art in the southern suns, he became susceptible to adventures of the flesh "and suffered unspeakably thereby." The reason is simply that "his heart was dead and without love."

When he leaves Munich after the conversation with Lisabeta, he does not return to Italy but instead goes back home to the north, to Denmark and Lübeck. There he will find those he had loved, to whom his heart had belonged, and who had brought him sadness and pain— but living emotions. Even on the boat going over to Denmark in the storm, his heart is alive. For that reason he cannot formulate the poem in which he tries to express his feelings. "But it got no further, he did not finish it. It was not fated to receive a final form nor in tranquillity to be welded to a perfect whole. For his heart was too full. . . ."[65]

In the calm, straightforward manner in which this is expressed, we feel Kröger's acceptance of his inevitable fate: that when his heart is full and alive, he cannot expect to be able to work out and formulate a theme. The sense of struggle and torment that had formerly been associated with the phrase "his heart was full" has gone.[66] He is aware that this direct feeling will give value to his work in the end, because it gives meaning to his life. The same acceptance of this fact is implied when the phrase appears again, when he sees his loves once more (though they are a new Hans and Inge) and the emotions of his boyhood return with the same power as before.

Yes, all was as it had been, and he too was happy, just as he had been. For his heart was alive. But between that past and this present what had happened to make him become that which he now was? Icy desolation, solitude: mind, and art, forsooth![67]

So, in his final letter to Lisabeta, he writes:

"I admire those proud, cold beings who adventure upon the paths of great and dæmonic beauty and despise 'mankind'; but I do not envy them. For if anything is capable of making a poet of a literary man, it is my *bourgeois* love of the human, the living and usual."[68]

In this love of life, which he hopes will mean his salvation as an artist, there is apparent a desperate and insistent assertion of values more valid than our critical and intellectual experience. This assertion

---

[65] *Ibid.*, p. 121.
[66] Cf. Wilkinson, *op. cit.*
[67] *Stories*, p. 131.
[68] *Ibid.*, p. 132.

of values parallels Nietzsche's struggle against the nihilistic trends of his own thought. One passage in Kröger's speech makes a reference to this parallel, while emphasizing a distinction between Kröger's love of everyday life and the violent dogmas of Nietzsche's philosophy.

"I love life...."

"But I implore you not to take what I am saying for literature. Don't think of Cæsar Borgia or any drunken philosophy that has him for a standard-bearer. He is nothing to me, your Cæsar Borgia. I have no opinion of him, and I shall never comprehend how one can honour the extraordinary and dæmonic as an ideal."[69]

Nietzsche, in reaction against the destructive negation to which all his thought seemed to lead, had turned to frantic denials of the mind and intellect and had called out in extravagant eulogies of the "man of prey" as the healthiest of all men. *"Caesar Borgia as Pope.... This would have been the triumph which I alone am longing for today."*[70] "The beast of prey and the man of prey (for instance, Caesar Borgia) are fundamentally misunderstood ... so long as one seeks a 'morbidness' in the constitution of these healthiest of all tropical monsters and growths."[71] Nietzschean disciples had extracted these pleas for a "healthy," antimoral superman, and had built a creed around the idea of savage and demonic greatness. It is true that the "superman" often lent itself to this interpretation, however inadequate it is as an appreciation of Nietzsche's work as a whole.

Kröger describes his love for life as a longing for the commonplace, the seductive banality of the everyday. The blond and blue-eyed Hans and Inge, who represent this healthy normality, can only by humorous implication be associated with Nietzsche's "blond beast," this "beast of prey hiding in all noble spirits" which at times "must get loose again";[72] nevertheless, despite all differences, we may question whether this longing for normality is not just as much a reaction against the mind as Nietzsche's superman. In just the same way it is a "self-betrayal" of the intellect in favor of unreasoning, simple, and direct life.

Whether this is true or not, Mann's rejection of the "drunken philosophy" of Caesar Borgia does not imply a rejection of Nietzsche. What he rejects is such an interpretation of Nietzsche's work. In *A Sketch of My Life,* Mann explains he had always held himself scornfully aloof from the "fashionable doctrines which had their origin in Nietzsche; the cult of superman, the easy 'renaissanceism,' the Caesar

[69] *Ibid.,* pp. 107–108.
[70] 16, pp. 228–229.
[71] 12, p. 118.
[72] 13, p. 40.

Borgia aesthetics, all the blood-and-beauty mouthings then in vogue."[73]
On the contrary, what he saw in Nietzsche, he said, was the psychologist of decadence, standing, like Mann himself, between decadence
and health.[74] Both Nietzsche and Mann struggle to oppose in themselves elements they feel as decadent. This side of Nietzsche finds expression most clearly in the preface to *The Case of Wagner*.

I am just as much a child of my age as Wagner—i.e. I am a decadent. The only
difference is that I recognized the fact, that I struggled against it. My greatest
preoccupation hitherto has been the problem of *decadence*, and I had reasons
for this. "Good and evil" form only a playful subdivision of this problem. If one
has trained one's eyes to detect the symptoms of decline, one also understands
morality,—one understands what lies concealed beneath its holiest names and
tables of values: e.g., *impoverished* life, the will to nonentity, great exhaustion.
Morality *denies* life ... In order to undertake such a mission I was obliged to exercise self-discipline: I had to side against all that was morbid in myself including Wagner, including Schopenhauer, including the whole of modern *humanity*.[75]

All three elements—impoverished life, the will to reach an end, the
great weariness—and at the same time the urge to resist them, are
found in Tonio Kröger.

---

[73] P. 22.
[74] *Observations*, pp. 47, 62.
[75] 8, pp. xxix–xxx.

# IV. TRISTAN

TRISTAN, THE OTHER long story in the collection published in 1903, is also concerned with the problem of the artist. The hero, Detlev Spinell, is involved in the same conflicts as Kröger, and Spinell's fate can best be interpreted through an understanding of Kröger's struggles. Spinell too suffers from the world and seeks a retreat in his art. But he fails to face the problem of Kröger's life—that of establishing a valid basis for the development of his work. He does not compromise, he does not attempt after his first novel to come to any easy reconciliation with the world. He struggles to pursue his art. For this reason we feel sympathy with him, and find pity for his sufferings. But he can make no advance. At last it has to be recognized that in his isolation he can be no more than the parody of a poet. He again is seeking only an escape from life, a retreat into the realm of his imagination he has created in response to his own needs. His work is consequently barren and meaningless; it does not serve for more than a means of revenge against a harsh and insensitive world. Once more Mann's set of values point to Nietzsche, and the explanation of Spinell's failure is involved in the lessons Mann drew from the philosopher.

Spinell lives in a sanatorium—as a protection from the world, not because he is sick. Here he can work in peace, unaffected by the demands and pressures outside. He has no friends, and holds himself aloof from the other patients. At times, however, the sight of something exceptionally beautiful rouses him to the expression of his feelings; then in his ardor he may be so carried away by emotion that he throws his arms around the neck of anyone who happens to be near. " 'How beautiful!' he would say, with his head on one side, his shoulders raised, his hands spread out, his lips and nostrils curled and distended. 'My God! look, how beautiful!' "[1]

This same precious manner is reflected in the one novel he has written. The scene is set in fashionable salons and luxurious boudoirs, and he has spent the most loving care on the descriptions of this delicate and overrefined world. Still, although he is an author by profession and seems to spend most of his time writing, he has not brought out another book. This is hardly surprising; what, after all, remains for him to say?

To the sanatorium comes Gabriele Klöterjahn, accompanied by her husband. She is delicate and weak, and seems languid and sadly

---

[1] *Stories*, pp. 138–139.

withdrawn from the concerns of the world. Her husband, by contrast, is a noisy, vigorous, energetic, self-confident, and assertive business-man who bursts in on the quiet of the sanatorium "Einfried." He can stay only long enough to make arrangements for his wife, because he has other interests to take him back to the life outside: his business and his young, flourishing child, at whose birth his wife had lost so much in vitality and strength. The very sound of the name "Klöter-jahn" suggests coarseness and vulgarity, whereas "Gabriele" by contrast conveys lightness and delicacy. Everything about the man breathes of healthy, unhypocritical self-satisfaction. His son too, we hear, is astonishingly healthy. He eats and drinks heartily, cries with his full lungs, and in every way surrenders himself to his instincts with an easy freedom that suggests his future assurance.

Spinell shows great interest in Gabriele and talks to her with im-mense consideration and reverence in a carefully subdued voice, which contrasts with the robust kindness of her husband. But she is de-votedly attached to Klöterjahn, and insists to Spinell that it was she who had determined on the marriage although her father had opposed it. We are led to believe that some healthy instinct had brought her to escape from her father's house and the duets they had been used to play together. Thomas Buddenbrook's wife Gerda too escaped from the confines of her artistic home, but her instinct was scarcely a healthy one, since the other, hidden side of Thomas seems to have appealed to her.

Spinell is shocked at Gabriele's marriage, and tries to arouse in her an awareness of her superiority of taste and subtlety. Her illness must be an expression of this; she cannot adapt herself to the life of a man like Klöterjahn. He imagines romantic scenes of her child-hood—she a queen among her companions—and seems to bring her to acquiesce in this idyll of the past.

The turning point of the Novelle occurs on a day of festivities when most of the patients have gone out on a sleigh ride. Gabriele and Spinell stay behind. He persuades her once more to play the piano, as she had hardly done since the days with her father, although she has been expressly forbidden to do so by the physician. She plays in a way that answers his hopes and apparently justifies his claims on her. At first she plays some Chopin nocturnes and then passages from *Tristan und Isolde,* the score of which he finds, as if by chance, lying on the piano. Mann, to recapture the mood of this music, interweaves his description with phrases from the text of the opera. She plays the opening prelude and then, in the twilight of the winter afternoon, the "Liebesnacht" of the second act:

O night of love, sink downwards and enfold them, grant them the oblivion they crave, release them from this world of partings and betrayals. Lo, the last light is quenched. Fancy and thought alike are lost, merged in the mystic shade that spread its wings of healing above their madness and despair. "Now, when deceitful daylight pales, when my raptured eye grows dim, then all that from which the light of day would shut my sight, seeking to blind me with false show, to the stanchless torments of my longing soul—then, ah, then, O wonder of fulfilment, even then I am the world!"[2]

The lovers lose themselves as in an eternal night of love, and seek release from the need of reawaking.

As it did for Hanno Buddenbrook, the music of Wagner expresses most poignantly the desire for release and harmony, "the longing for holy night." This night of love has no suggestion of a future life created in it, but it is the expression of an erotic longing for ungraspable beauty, for a joy of union that means the end of all individual suffering and struggle.

Nietzsche says of *Tristan*, in his early essay "Richard Wagner in Bayreuth" (from *Thoughts Out of Season*).

The real "opus metaphysicum" of all art, a work upon which rests the broken look of a dying man with his insatiable and sweet craving for the secrets of night and of death, far away from life which throws a horribly spectral morning light, sharply, upon all that is evil, delusive and sundering.[3]

In beautiful and sensitive prose he describes the release that *Tristan* brought after the miseries of daily life:

Has not a haven been found for all wanderers on high and desert seas, and has not peace settled over the face of the waters? Must not he who leaves these spheres of ruling profundity and loneliness for the very differently ordered world with its plains and lower levels, cry continually like Isolde: "Oh, how could I bear it? How can I still bear it?"[4]

As already discussed, Mann insisted that Nietzsche never overcame his love for *Tristan und Isolde,* which always aroused in the philosopher a nostalgic longing for the past. But Nietzsche revolted against the "dangerous fascination" of what he thought was the ultimately morbid and degenerate quality of this music. "Tristan—the metaphysical directed against life."[5] This work, which he maintains is the

---

[2] *Ibid.*, p. 154.
[3] 4, p. 165.
[4] 4, p. 126.
[5] Not included in the English edition. German Musarion edition, vii, p. 365. "Preliminary sketches for *Richard Wagner in Bayreuth, 1875–76.*"

most characteristic of Wagner's achievements, is for that reason also
the most dangerous. "This work is without question Wagner's 'non
plus ultra'; after its creation, the composition of *The Mastersingers*
and of the *Ring* was a relaxation to him. To become more healthy—
this in a nature like Wagner's amounts to going backwards."[6] For
Mann there can be no doubt, though he is aware that certain critics
have disputed the idea,[7] that *Tristan* has its origins in Wagner's reading of Schopenhauer and that it expresses in the most alluring form
Schopenhauer's metaphysical escape from the wheel of Ixion, the
domination of the will. In discussing this relationship in a speech on
Wagner written in 1933, Mann quotes a letter from Wagner to Ma-
thilde Wesendonck. Wagner wrote, from Paris in 1860: "Often I
look with yearning towards the land of Nirwana. But Nirwana soon
becomes Tristan again."[8]

If we are to survive the seduction of this music, Mann will argue,
our longing for love and eternity must be countered by the moral
discipline that hardens us for life. Spinell has no power to resist the
seduction of this longing for eternal beauty. Yet if he succumbs, he
is denying life itself.

After this episode Gabriele's illness, which had seemed trivial, is
found to be very serious. All remedies are tried in vain. The doctors
give up hope, and Klöterjahn is recalled. Spinell feels impelled to
explain what has happened and, although Klöterjahn is under the
same roof, writes Gabriele's husband a long and elaborate letter.

Here in a letter he can find revenge, give expression to his hatred
for Klöterjahn, who represents in his eyes the triumphant dullness
of ordinary life.

"Kindly permit me to tell you, sir, that I hate you. I hate you and your child,
as I hate the life of which you are the representative: cheap, ridiculous, but yet
triumphant life, the everlasting antipodes and deadly enemy of beauty."[9]

In Gabriele's death alone will she find an escape from the lowering
power of common everyday existence "in the service of that stupid,
contemptible, clumsy graven image we call nature." Spinell recognizes he is the weaker:

"You are stronger than I. I have no armour for the struggle between us, I have

---

[6] 17, p. 44.
[7] Cf. the essay "Sufferings and Greatness of Richard Wagner," in *Essays of Three Decades*, p. 332.
[8] *Essays of Three Decades*, p. 334.
[9] *Stories*, p. 161.

only the Word, avenging weapon of the weak. Today I have availed myself of this weapon. This letter is nothing but an act of revenge . . ."[10]

His action in writing this letter, in which his overflowing hatred and despair must come out, is itself curiously reminiscent of Nietzsche's behavior after the Lou Salomé episode, when he too found escape from the misery of his experience in violent letters of complaint and abuse, first to his sister, then to Lou herself, and finally to Lou's and his own friend Paul Rée. There is indeed a close parallel, which Mann may have had in mind, between Spinell and Nietzsche, the hermit of Sils-Maria, who suddenly believed he had found in Lou an understanding soul. Compare, for example, extracts from the draft of a final letter to Lou from Nietzsche:

But Lou, what kind of letters are you writing to me! Only little vindictive school-girls write in this way. What have I to do with these miserable trivialities. Understand that I want you to raise yourself in my esteem, not to make yourself smaller. How can I forgive you if I can't first rediscover in you that nature which alone makes forgiveness possible at all.

How impoverished your humanity seems in comparison with that of friend Rée! How poor in honor, in gratitude, in piety, in civility, in admiration, in modesty—not to speak of higher matters. What would you answer if I asked you: Are you honorable? Are you incapable of treachery?

Do you have no comprehension of how much self-denial a man like I has need of when he is near you. You have had to do with one of the most patient and well-meaning of men, but please note that against all petty self-seekers and pleasure-hunters I need no other argument but disgust.[11]

Compare also the draft of a letter to Paul Rée written in intense fury in the summer of 1883, although it was then months after the events he is discussing:

Almost a year too late I received information about the part you played in the events of last summer; and I have never felt such complete disgust in my soul as I do now at the thought that a person so sneaking, lying and cunning could have passed for years as my friend. . . . So the vilification of my character originates with you, and Fräulein Salomé was only the spokesman, the vile spokesman, of your thoughts about me. Now indeed I understand better this whole business which almost cost me my life and which has almost estranged me from those people closest to me and most worthy of my respect. . . .

I would take great delight in giving you a lesson in practical morality with a few bullets; and perhaps with the best of luck I would succeed in once and for all rendering you incapable of any occupation with problems of morals. . . .[12]

---

[10] *Ibid.*

[11] Elizabeth Förster-Nietzsche, *Life of Nietzsche*, vol. ii, pp. 139 ff.

[12] Erich Podach, *Friedrich Nietzsche und Lou Salomé*, pp. 84 ff.; *Gesammelte Briefe*, vol. 5, pp. 524 ff.

Significantly, this letter was not sent. Instead Nietzsche wrote to Paul Rée's brother Georg. This letter too is dated "Summer, 1883."

Our short acquaintance at Leipzig must be my justification for writing to you today something that I may not write to your brother Paul—namely that all further contact between him and me would be below my dignity. Only now, almost a year too late, vulgar, miserable facts come to my knowledge which compromise your brother irredeemably before me . . .[13]

The similarity in tone of these letters to Spinell's is striking. There are the same psychological tension, the same passionate expression of anger and despair that had been so long concealed.

When Klöterjahn receives Spinell's note, he angrily comes to see him. Spinell cuts a poor figure in the ensuing argument, and is completely overwhelmed by the contemptuous fury of his enemy. Only the announcement that Gabriele is on the brink of death interrupts the scene, and Spinell escapes into the garden. Even here he runs into Klöterjahn's happy, plump-cheeked son sitting in his perambulator. For some reason the child begins to roar with laughter at the sight of Spinell, and Spinell cannot face him.

Herr Spinell turned round and went thence. Pursued by the youthful Klöterjahn's joyous screams, he went away across the gravel, walking stiffly, yet not without grace; his gait was the hesitating gait of one who would disguise the fact that, inwardly, he is running away.[14]

On the day when Klöterjahn comes to see him, Spinell has slept late and as a result is heavy-headed, nervous, and incapable of putting up a fight. His normal practice is to get up early, as he tells Gabriele, precisely because it is his natural inclination to lie in bed. Conscience makes this demand on him; his type of person, he says, works hard in order to swindle his conscience into feeling pleased and satisfied. A certain control is essential; to get up early, to take a cold bath, and to go out walking in the snow are a discipline that gives him a sense of self-satisfaction. Spinell requires the order of his daily regime, just as he requires the brightness and hardness, the austere simplicity and strength of the Empire furnishings among which he lives, for these too, as he says, are morally elevating to him.

Gabriele calls this discipline self-conquest, self-abnegation. This is in part a commonplace comment, a nicely comforting expression, which is emphasized by the way it is introduced. The word is reëchoed by

---

[13] Podach, *op. cit.*, pp. 86 ff.; *Gesammelte Briefe*, vol. 5, pp. 524 ff.
[14] *Stories*, p. 166.

the simple Frau Spatz, Gabriele's constant companion, who is present at their talk. Spinell is asserting:

"My getting up early is all hypocrisy, believe me."

"Why do you say that, Herr Spinell? On the contrary, I call it self-abnegation." Frau Spatz, too, called it self-abnegation.[15]

The expression—in German "Selbstüberwindung"—is not altogether lacking a serious meaning that points to its use in Nietzsche. Spinell's discipline can very well be related to Mann's concept of Nietzsche's "self-conquest." Spinell gains a certain temporary victory over himself. He is able to overcome to some degree his sense of futility and uncertainty. He does not succumb to the temptation to "lie in bed and despair," or to the danger of surrendering merely to the expansion of his feelings. In this daily regime there is an element of the discipline with which Mann himself struggled to control the urge to relaxation and disintegration within. Mann has stressed that it was this very aspect of Nietzsche—Nietzsche the self-conqueror—that concerned him. It is the Nietzsche who made war on himself, who rejected all that he loved and all that brought him ease and comfort if he felt it led to decay and the denial of life, who renounced all that he most desired in order to seek standards that affirmed life. In *A Sketch of My Life*, Mann says: "In a word, what I saw in Nietzsche above all else was the victor over self."[16]

Self-conquest meant for Nietzsche a victory over comforting illusions, however appealing; it was the capacity to reject any pretense that might provide a false support. It was also a quality that provided tenacity of purpose and gave him the strength to maintain himself in the search for knowledge, although that knowledge seemed to lead nowhere. "My *strongest* characteristic is self-conquest. But I need it most,—I am always at the abyss."[17]

But self-conquest for Nietzsche can be only a means to prepare us for the battle of life. We recognize our true needs and make sacrifices accordingly. Self-conquest has value only if it is directed toward a higher end. This is the meaning of two apothegms from the time of *Zarathustra*:

All virtue and self-conquest has meaning only as a preparation for *mastering . . .*[18]

---

[15] *Ibid.*, p. 142.

[16] P. 22.

[17] Not included in the English edition. German Musarion edition, xxi, p. 102. "Comments from the period of *Zarathustra* and *Joyful Wisdom*, 1881–83."

[18] Not included in the English edition. German Musarion edition, xiv, p. 125. "From the period of *Zarathustra*, 1882–86."

*All virtue* and *self-conquest* has no meaning at all except as a means for the development of *one's power of mastery*.[19]

We overcome lesser desires in response to the overriding demands of our will to power. The character of Savonarola in *Fiorenza* shows Mann's interpretation of this: the sacrifice of temporary personal comforts for the attainment of a higher goal, in him the authority of the "ascetic priest," which is the expression of the will to power itself.

Spinell has no such overriding ambition. His discipline has no basis in a work that is all-important to him. He is far too skeptical to believe in any illusions of that kind. He sees his self-conquest as mere play acting. He tells Gabriele it is simply hypocrisy, a pretense to give meaning to his life. He is only trying to silence his bad conscience behind this discipline. He knows that his aesthetic denials of worldly values expresses only the hatred for life that he admitted in the letter to Klöterjahn—the "triumphant life" that is the enemy of all beauty. But what is left if beauty does not serve life but conveys only a longing for death?

The question arises whether, without any such fanatical ambition as Savonarola is to show, and in awareness of the relativity of his aims, a man may establish a basis for moral resolution that will give a meaning to his life. It was Nietzsche who put this question before Mann, and it was Nietzsche's search to establish such a discipline in face of the most complex appreciation of the metaphysical and psychological difficulties that attracted Mann. This problem becomes more and more prominent in Mann's next works—above all in *Death in Venice*—but it is already suggested in the implied contrast between Spinell's failure and the achievement of Dr. Leander, the director of the sanatorium.

Dr. Leander despises Spinell, and makes an effort to convey his dislike for the author who is among his guests. When Gabriele asks about Spinell on her arrival, Dr. Leander replies:

"Yes...I really don't know....He writes...I believe he has written a book, some sort of novel. I really don't know what."

By which Dr. Leander conveyed that he had no great opinion of the author and declined all responsibility on the score of him.[20]

This is emphasized a few lines later when Spinell asks about the new

---

[19] Not included in the English edition. German Musarion edition, xiv, p. 116. "From the period of *Zarathustra*, 1882–86."

[20] *Stories*, p. 140.

arrivals and Dr. Leander answers him abruptly. "For he set no great store by the author."[21]

Dr. Leander is a melancholy, yet controlled and disciplined man. He has the look of a man whom knowledge has "cooled and hardened and filled with silent forbearing pessimism." In his own way he holds his patients under his control.

And with this beard, these lenses, this look, and in his short, reserved, preoccupied way, he holds his patients in his spell: holds those sufferers who, too weak to be laws unto themselves, put themselves into his hands that his severity may be a shield unto them.[22]

He is able to provide strength for his patients through laws that will help them to life. But we do not know how real his strength is, or whether it too may not spring from self-deception.

---

[21] *Ibid.*
[22] *Ibid.*, p. 133.

# V. FIORENZA

In *Tonio Kröger* and *Tristan,* Mann had achieved a synthesis of his early themes. When these stories were completed, he turned more freely to subjects outside his own personal experience. The principal works of the next few years—*Fiorenza, Royal Highness,* and *Felix Krull*—introduce a wealth of new material and interests.

In his final letter to Lisabeta, Tonio Kröger had promised that in his future work he would give form to the unborn world of human figures he dimly saw waiting to be ordered and shaped.

"The work I have so far done is nothing or not much—as good as nothing. I will do better, Lisabeta—this is a promise. As I write, the sea whispers to me and I close my eyes. I am looking into a world unborn and formless, that needs to be ordered and shaped; I see into a whirl of shadows of human figures who beckon to me to weave spells to redeem them..."[1]

In *Fiorenza* (1904), Mann's only attempt at a drama, he comes as close perhaps as he ever did to fulfilling Kröger's promise. Here Mann attempts to put on the stage the whole panorama of the Florentine Renaissance during its decline at the time of the death of Lorenzo de' Medici and the rise to power of the fanatical Savonarola. It can scarcely be said that Mann succeeds here—if that was his intention—in presenting a world of human people, living creatures of flesh and blood. The protagonists never become much more than abstractions representing carefully graded and explicitly distinguished points of view. In the *Observations,*[2] Mann regrets that all his attempts had failed to give the work a less theoretic and more personal and intimate character. *Fiorenza* is hardly to be studied as a drama, but rather perhaps as a dramatic dialogue that, in its abundance of intellectual argument and thought, foreshadows *The Magic Mountain.*

Although Mann no longer presents his problems in personal terms, the conflicts of *Fiorenza* are an extension of those in *Tonio Kröger* and closely involved with them. He is, as it were, broadening the context, elaborating further consequences of his position. An appreciation of these conflicts is essential to an understanding of Mann's development and his struggle to come to terms with himself. At the same time, because the personal element is absent and because the problems are raised to a universal level, the relationship to Nietzsche—already so important in *Tonio Kröger*—becomes all the more evident. The questions debated follow consistently from Nietzschean assumptions,

[1] *Stories,* p. 132.
[2] P. 64.

and can be interpreted only in the light of Nietzsche's thought. His influence appears everywhere.

The decline of the Florentine ideal is conceived in terms of nineteenth-century decadence. There is a close relation between the artists of the Medici court and those of Tonio Kröger's Munich. In fact the main theme of *Fiorenza* had been anticipated in one of the short stories of the *Tristan* collection—*Gladius Dei,* written in 1902, which is set in the Munich of the *fin de siècle.* Several references to Florence and the Medicis suggest that Mann was even then considering a study of that age as the classic example of the problem with which he was concerned. A young man objects to the picture of a Madonna displayed in the window of a bookstore. He begs the owner to remove this image of the Holy Mother because it portrays her with a worldly and physical, even lustful, attraction. It is quite simply a picture of the artist's mistress. What has this erotic, sensual art to do with the Mother of God?

This conflict between morality and art is the subject of *Fiorenza,* for included under art are to be understood all that gives aesthetic pleasure to life—beauty, grace, style, joy in living. Under the Medicis, Florence has made the world richer and more desirable than it has ever been before, and filled it with beauty and an ever greater fascination of wit and brilliance. Man has learned to brush aside everything sad, ugly, or painful, and to keep his soul receptive to only the beautiful and joyous. Yet in the midst of this luxury there rises a burning hatred for a life that seeks only the refinements of pleasure at the cost of all purity and moral value. Savonarola enflames the heart of Florence in preaching redemption from this vain, self-indulgent pleasure seeking. God requires of us self-denial, self-abnegation, liberation from the sensual and earthly. In the search for beauty we are in danger of losing our souls. This revolt has already been presented in *Gladius Dei.* The young man thrown out of the Munich bookstore does not see the people laughing at him. He has a vision that through him the vanities of the world, which the portrait of the Madonna represents, will be destroyed.

For what he beheld upon the mosaic pavement before the great loggia were all the vanities of this world: the masked costumes of the artist balls, the decorations, vases and art objects, the nude statues, the female busts, the picturesque rebirths of the pagan age, the portraits of famous beauties by the hands of masters, the elegantly bound erotic verse, the art brochures—all these he saw heaped in a pyramid and going up in crackling flames amid loud exaltations from the people enthralled by his own frightful words.[3]

[3] *Stories,* p. 193.

Mann presents to us a Florence on the verge of its decline. The arts still flourish as the natural product of an overflowing creative genius, but tastes have become too subtle, too cultured, and too refined for the spontaneous joy in beauty to be still easily found. This new state of mind—an extreme sensibility, self-indulgent but unsatisfied— is represented by Pico della Mirandola. He is a scholar and humanist, poet and man of letters. We admire the perfect style and manner of his speech, the "harmony and taste of his periods"; but he is the product of too complex a society, he is too educated and disciplined, too cultured and instructed, to live joyously or creatively. He finds certain pleasures in the beauty of a particularly well formed chair or spoon or in an artistically prepared meal. But it is a passive aestheti- cism—he always looks outside for new sources of excitement and new thrills. He "looks for shivers," as the young Giovanni de' Medici says. To him Savonarola is a new fascination. It is Pico who has discovered this barbaric preacher and introduced him to Florence. He rejoices that it is now the fashion to listen to Savonarola's sermons and to be deeply affected by them, that it has become the height of good taste to abjure the world and enter a monastery.

Beside Pico more modest men continue to represent the traditions of the Florentine culture. Poliziano, the tutor of Lorenzo de' Medici's son Giovanni, is the perfect figure of the poet-humanist, scholar, and man of taste, the inheritor of the classical culture and its exponent. He is happy to be living in this golden age, he says, which is like a new-blooming flower. Yet at the same time he is slightly comic and pedantic. He is gently ridiculed by his pupil. It is his somewhat ludicrous ambition to have Plato canonized. His point of view is too simple; his convictions, Pico suggests, are almost as one-sided as Savonarola's—he too sees things from one single aspect. Poliziano is a forerunner of Settembrini and Dr. Zeitblom, the attractive but slightly simple and too easily optimistic scholar and humanist.

Also to represent the glory of Florence are the whole crowd of artists. These comic—even rather absurd—figures, quarrelsome, child- ish, egoistic, are nevertheless immensely gifted and fill the halls of Florence with an astonishing wealth of beauty. In their very childish- ness, as in the spontaneity and joyfulness of their art, there is the exact opposite of decadence. What comprehension could these men have, for example, of Kröger's fate? How could they understand his bitter lesson that good work occurs only under the pressure of an unhappy life, that a man must die to life in order to be a true creator?

The Florentines' art comes easily, springing from overflowing gifts. But Mann is not concerned with the conditions of a "healthier" age. The work of these artists has lost any genuine meaning because it no longer corresponds to the real needs of the time. Their art leaves unused too much blood, too much virility. They aim simply at the enrichment of our pleasures. But this no longer seems enough. They put the same devotion into the plans for a carnival as they accord to a silver spoon or to a painting. Indeed, in a certain sense Grifone, the carnival designer, is their most representative figure. But in his work too things have symbolically reached a climax. Though one carnival has just ended, another is about to begin and Grifone is desperate for a new idea. On the last occasion he had invented the much-admired "Procession of the Dead," with corpses arising from their coffins. What idea will not be an anticlimax after the "Procession of the Dead," which, after so many highly colored carnivals, had had the effect of a savory after too much sweet?

In contrast to this world stand the two heroes who vie for the favors of Florence—Lorenzo and Savonarola. Lorenzo, the representative of the Renaissance in its glory, is seen as the mighty hero, a man of immense talents, whose life is a triumph, a great flame blazing boldly and royally to the skies. Pico tells how Lorenzo might spend his day:

Perhaps in the forenoon you may have been working out a new law for the statutes, designed to give power more fully into your hands, that you might be in a position to bless Florence still more freely with beauty and joy; perhaps uttered the death sentence on some noble adversary; argued in the Platonic Academy upon virtue, presided over a symposium in a group of artists and lovely women; at table solved theoretic questions in art and poetry—and in all that you had brought your whole mind to bear and now were sharing the evening play of our minds, as fresh and detached as though you had not given out any part of your vital energy.[4]

Lorenzo's followers cannot understand his illness—they complain of the doctors, and suggest some enemy's slow-working poison as a cause— but it is clear that Lorenzo, like Mann's other heroes, is not a strong man. He is not great because of overflowing strength; instead he is a man of infirmity and weakness, great only through the force of his will, who has worn away his energy in the constant demands he has made on himself. Pierleoni cannot describe the nature of his disease except in the significant phrase: "The marrow of life itself is attacked by decay."[5]

It is not in possession or ability alone that greatness lies, but in

[4] *Ibid.*, p. 241.
[5] *Ibid.*, p. 201.

the force of our desires. "Longing is a giant's power; owning unmans," Lorenzo says. "Whither the longing urges, there one is not, that one is not. . . . And yet man likes to confuse himself with his longing."[6] Lorenzo is called the lord of beauty, but he himself is ugly. He adores all that appeals to his senses, but to him one sense—that of smell—is lacking. He is in fact a cripple—and not only in his body, it is suggested. Yet he has compelled the frenzy and passion within him to follow a measure and rhythm.

Without my longing I should be but a satyr; and when my poets put me with the company of the Olympians, not one of them dreams of the long, stern discipline which went to bridle my wild nature. It was well so. Had I been born beautiful, I had never made myself the lord of beauty. Hindrance is the will's best friend.[7]

Lorenzo's achievements are the fruit of his discipline and control. His body is consumed by the demands he imposes upon it. Without hesitation he expends his energy to struggle after his own ambitions. An inner force impels him to this wild, brief, burning life. The hero for Mann is never merely the strong. So Piero de' Medici, Lorenzo's son, is doomed to failure. For him the possession of the glory—the unchallenged power of the tyrant, at best the satisfaction of exercising his talents—is sufficient. When he seeks to woo Fiore, Lorenzo's mistress, she dismisses him.

Fiore: You are no hero; you are only strong. And you bore me.
Piero: Only strong? Only strong? And is not the strong man a hero?
Fiore: No. He who is weak, but of so glowing a spirit that even so he wears the garland—he is a hero.[8]

Fiore, the talented, beautiful mistress of Lorenzo, is also something more—the embodiment of Florence herself. Lorenzo has won her, but a new hero arises to challenge him; not Piero, the heir to the Medicis, but Savonarola, who singles her out for his attacks. For she sees this abuse as a new form of wooing, a new excitement, as appealing to her as to all Florence, an escape, a new stimulation for a jaded and licentious taste. It is revealed that in his youth Savonarola too had felt the passion of desire for Fiore; but he was sullen, weak, ugly, buried in his work, a source of amusement to her and her friends. She had repulsed him, and he had fled into the cloister. Out of this rejection new energy had been aroused in Savonarola to propel him to fame and power. For Savonarola too is weak but of glowing spirit. His body is

[6] *Ibid.*, p. 268.
[7] *Ibid.*
[8] *Ibid.*, p. 235.

wracked by dysentery and fever aroused through constant watching and fasting, but the same fire that burns in Lorenzo impels him to the pulpit.

The dying Lorenzo finds no comfort in his court to satisfy his tortures and doubts. He seeks consolation with his artists and with his Platonist philosophers, but finds none. Why not? Because they are not his sort. "They admire me, perhaps, they love me, and they know nothing of me. Courtiers, orators, children—what use is all that to me?"[9] Accordingly he sends for Savonarola to hear his confession— not as a priest to whom he will submit, but as an equal, a man who has risen up beside him—so that together they may feel the nature of the power that works in them, that they may recognize that in their inextinguishable longing for the heights they are separated from other men.

For a moment when these two heroes meet it would seem that the conflict that had divided them—purity and redemption on the one hand, and beauty and art on the other—is to collapse. They see that behind their work lies the controlling force of the will to power. They seem to unite in a comprehension for the power they share, in a scorn for the masses they dominate.

Lorenzo: That you grew great in Florence was only because this Florence is so free, such a spoilt child of art, as to take you as her lord. Were it less so, were it only a very little less lapped in art, it would tear you to pieces instead of paying you homage. You are aware of that?

The Prior: I will not be aware of it.

Lorenzo: May one will not to be aware? You rail at the indifference, at the refusal to see, at the shamelessness. But you are not yourself ashamed to win such power, knowing by what means you win it?

The Prior: I am chosen. I may know and still do it. For I must be strong. God performs miracles. You see in me the miracle of detachment regained. (*Looking at the bust of Cæsar*) Did *he* ask by what means he climbed?

Lorenzo: Cæsar? You are a monk. And you have ambition!

The Prior: How could I not have, I that suffered so? Ambition says: My sufferings must not have been in vain. They must bring me fame.

Lorenzo: By God, that is it! Have I not known it? You have understood all that to a miracle. We rulers of men are egoist, and they blame us for it, not knowing that it comes of our suffering. They call us hard and understand not it was pain made us so. We may justly say: Look at yourselves, who have had so much easier a time on this earth. To myself I am torment and joy sufficient.

The Prior: But they do not rail. They marvel. They reverence. See them come to the strong ego, the many who are only *we,* see them serve, see them tirelessly do his will—

Lorenzo: Although his own advantage is plain to any eye—

---

[9] *Ibid.*, p. 265.

The Prior: Although he leave their services quite unrewarded and take them for granted—[10]

For a moment they are united in this dithyramb of power, but the direction that the will takes cannot be ignored. Savonarola sees his mission as the service of God. He rejects Lorenzo as a brother in power, and denounces the evil that Lorenzo has worked. When Lorenzo asks what evil means in this sense, he replies: "All that is against spirit within us and without." Spirit means the triumph over the fleshly and the worldly. All that Lorenzo has achieved has been to enhance the allurements of the world. In this reply Lorenzo sees the inevitability of their clash. What Savonarola seeks in the victory of the spirit over the worldly is the victory of death—eternal peace from strife. Savonarola speaks cryptically of breaking the wings—a phrase that is repeatedly mentioned—and Lorenzo sees that the wings he means are the wings of life itself. "It is death whom you proclaim as spirit, and all the life of life is art."[11] The fire that the monk has fanned is the fire of destruction, and Fiore cries to him in the last moments of the play: "Cease to will, instead of willing nothingness!" What he wills in the name of the spirit, what he calls purity and freedom, is at bottom redemption from the world. Yet, we are to understand, this will itself is dependent upon the force of the normal positive impulses of life in man.

In all this discussion we feel the influence of Nietzsche immediately below the surface. In the *Observations*, Mann declares:

The title was no less symbolic than that of the artist Novelle [*Tonio Kröger*], and it denotes that which was personal and original in this attempt at a song in a higher key; here is heard a youthful, lyrical song to fame,—joy in fame and fear of it,—felt by one who had been ensnared by success and embraced by the world at a tender age. "O world, O profoundest joy! The lover's dream of power, sweeter, more consuming! ... One should not possess, longing is a giant's power, but possession unmans! The rest is Nietzsche.[12]

The will to power as the governing principle of men's actions is a basic doctrine in Nietzsche. Zarathustra says:

Wherever I found a living thing, there found I Will to Power; and even in the will of the servant found I the will to be master.[13]

Only where there is life, is there also will: not, however, Will to Life, but—so I teach thee—Will to Power![14]

[10] *Ibid.*, p. 269.
[11] *Ibid.*, p. 271.
[12] P. 64.
[13] 11, p. 136.
[14] 11, p. 137.

For Nietzsche, greatness lies in the strength of our desires, which means ultimately the intensity of our will to power. But it seems that the will to power must be properly used and recognized. It is a valid force only when it is used positively to heighten our desire for life. "The question is, how far an opinion is life-furthering, life-preserving, species-preserving, perhaps species-rearing. . . ."[15]

In his appeal to Savonarola, Lorenzo de' Medici affirms the nature of the force that is at work within them, and wishes to establish it as a living principle that guides all their apparent motives and that gives them superiority over other men. Greatness is falsely interpreted by Piero de' Medici, the tryant who scorns the people and seeks only the glory and unlimited authority of rulership. His doctrine—the worship of external strength and the ruthless display of power—is one wrongly ascribed to Nietzsche by some of his early followers. In the mere expression of strength lie the seeds of its own decay; true power lies in the struggle, and above all in the struggle within an individual—in the conquest of his own weakness. This is the way the Medicis have risen, according to Lorenzo.

We are not kings, not princes in Florence. We have no document on which our power is secured. We rule without a crown, by natural right, by our own strength. We became great of ourselves, by industry, by struggle, by self-discipline; the idle throng stood amazed and then submitted. But such power, my son, must daily be won afresh.[16]

Disillusioned in his son, Lorenzo tries to establish recognition of the nature of the will in Savonarola, the only person he acknowledges as his equal. He suggests Savonarola must accept the true motives of his actions and seek values that are built on this acceptance. But Savonarola is unable to see—or refuses to see—the nature of this power. It is too strong within him; he is the unconscious vessel of its force. As such he is the embodiment of Nietzsche's "ascetic priest," who preaches redemption as a disguised means to obtaining the conditions for his own authority. Nietzsche's essay "What is the meaning of ascetic ideals?"[17] discusses exactly this question. Ascetic ideals mean different things in different people, but the fact of their constant recurrence is evidence of a fundamental characteristic of the human will, its "horror vacui." Man must have a goal. He is willing to sacrifice his comfort and his pleasure for the attainment of a purpose. He prefers to will nothingness than not will at all.[18] These words are the very same as

---

[15] 12, p. 8.
[16] *Stories*, p. 249.
[17] 13, p. 121.
[18] *Ibid.*

those used by Fiore, symbol of Florence, in the last lines of the play. "Cease to will, instead of willing nothingness. Void the power! Renounce! Be a monk!"[19] And the whole of Nietzsche's essay is an explanation of what he means by "willing nothingness," and hence can serve as a commentary on Savonarola's character itself.

Man does not seek happiness as such. He needs to find a road in which his instinctive capacities can come to fruition. Every animal strives by instinct for an optimum of favorable conditions in which it is free to discharge its power fully and attain its maximum consciousness of power. It does not seek its road to happiness, but its road to power—to action, to mightiest action—and actually in most cases its road to unhappiness. For example, asceticism is the condition under which the philosopher lives most effectively; it is the condition for highest and keenest spirituality. Such a condition does not negate existence for the philosopher, but rather it is a means for his own existence—but only his own existence, and at the sacrifice of others. "Pereat mundus, fiat philosophia."

We know what are the three great catch-words of the ascetic ideal: poverty, humility, chastity; and now just look closely at the lives of all the great fruitful inventive spirits—you will always find again and again these three qualities. *Not for a minute*, as is self-evident, as though, perhaps, they were part of their virtues—what has this type of man to do with virtues?—but as the most essential and natural conditions of their *best* existence, their *finest* fruitfulness.[20]

This ascetic life is really a self-contradiction; it is an extraordinary example of what Nietzsche calls "ressentiment"—the resentment of insensate instinct and will to power that seeks to become master, not merely over some element in life, but over life itself, over the deepest, strongest, and most fundamental forces in life.

Here is an attempt made to utilise power to dam the sources of power; here does the green eye of jealousy turn even against physiological well-being, especially against the expression of such well-being, beauty, joy; while a sense of pleasure is experienced and *sought* in abortion, in decay, in pain, in misfortune, in ugliness, in voluntary punishment, in the exercising, flagellation, and sacrifice of the self.[21]

Suffering enjoys itself, and grows more and ever more confident in proportion as its presupposition—physiological vitality—diminishes.

Savonarola overcomes his own sensuality but, in preaching a flight from the world, thereby asserts his own power. What we learn through

---

[19] *Stories*, p. 272.
[20] 13, p. 137.
[21] 13, pp. 150–151.

Fiore of Savonarola's youth indicates that his entry into the cloister is a reaction against the health and vitality of his companions, in whose activities he cannot join. Whereas the company was talented, fortunate, and merry, he himself was shy and retiring; he would shut himself away on his own, bury himself in books and his own writings, or play mournful melodies on his lute. He was small and weak, ugly as darkness, contemptuous of the others, who would either ignore or tease him. At the same time the strength of his passions was disclosed in his desire for Fiore; and so in the cloister, where circumstances were beneficial to him, he grew great by the unheard-of power of his preaching. Yet what he preaches is hatred for the healthy and all lovers of joy and beauty, and therefore hatred for the very forces that make for life itself.

Until the present time, Nietzsche suggests, philosophy has had to appear in a disguised form. Philosophers have been regarded with deep mistrust, and find all valuations turned against them. Consequently contemplative men were compelled to establish their position through self-sacrifice and self-mortification. And this ascetic life came to serve as the condition of their existence. It came to be regarded as the philosophers' attitude as such. Is it possible, however, Nietzsche asks, that this state of affairs has changed, that the philosopher will now find the self-confidence to appear in his true form on earth? Will he find the freedom of will to teach without this ascetic disguise? Lorenzo appeals to Savonarola to recognize the origin from which his standards have come, and hence to seek to establish a more honest code of values built on the recognition of the true forces within him. Lorenzo is thus for the moment a prophet of Nietzsche's superman. Man needs a goal; superman provides a new aim on which man's ambitions can be set. For superman requires the affirmation of man's will as the force that leads to greatness.

Lo, I teach you the Superman!

The Superman is the meaning of the earth. Let your will say: The Superman *shall be* the meaning of the earth!

I conjure you my brethren, *remain true to the earth*, and believe not those who speak to you of superearthly hopes! Poisoners are they, whether they know it or not.[22]

Lorenzo, in the last few moments with Savonarola, sings feverishly the song of life:

Oh, my dreams! My power and art! Florence was my lyre. Did it not resound? Sweetly? It sang of my longing. It sang of beauty, it sang of great desire, it sang,

---

[22] 11, p. 7.

it sang the great song of life. . . . Hush! On your knees. . . . There! I see her. She comes, she draws near to me, all the veils fall and all my blood flows out to meet her naked beauty. Oh, joy! Oh, sweet and fearful thrill! Am I chosen to look upon you, Venus Genetrix, you who are life, the sweet world? . . . Creative beauty, mighty impulse of art! Venus Fiorenza![23]

But Savonarola rejects him; Lorenzo collapses, and Savonarola, confident in his strength, marches on to the assertion of his destiny.

The ascetic ideal preached by Savonarola aims at the negation of life—the state of being otherwise, of being elsewhere, in another world; but its appeal, Nietzsche argues, lies in the fact that it is really prompted by the self-protective instinct of life—degenerating life that seeks to maintain itself by all means. The very power of the priest's wishing binds him to life and makes him a tool for bringing about more favorable conditions for being here and for being a man. The priest by his power holds fast to existence the whole herd of the mis-fashioned, the disappointed, the maltreated, the defective—every type of sufferer from himself. He protects them from their self-contempt, justifies their sufferings. For it seems we are all in part malcontents, unable to rid ourselves of chagrin at self.[24]

Hence Savonarola's success with the crowds of Florence. His appeal is precisely for those who are unsuccessful—the outcasts, the defeated, those for whom the prosperity and well-being of others only emphasize their own failure. He makes life possible for them.

It must be emphasized that his appeal is not only to the rabble and the unsuccessful. He himself certainly is by no means a member of the mob. He comes from an old and highly respected Ferrarese family. Moreover, as Giovanni insists, he is a many-sided man, constitutionally sensitive in both mind and body. He has entered the despised men-dicant order and, by reason of his own gifts, overcome the prejudices against it and turned them into admiration. The order that he entered, casual and easy-going like many others, has become a model of piety and humility. His preaching is itself an art; and although he scorns the classical forms of oratory Poliziano demands, he makes all too skillful use of eloquence and rhetoric to arouse the highest pitch of emotion in his audience. The extent of his appeal indicates the under-lying insecurity of a wide circle of the Florentines. Not only the mob, but the aristocracy, even the fat bourgeoisie, are among his admirers. Young, talented, well-educated men from the best families take the

---

[23] *Stories*, p. 270.
[24] Cf. 13, pp. 152 ff.

cowl and enter the monasteries. Botticelli abandons his sensual art, and asserts that in the future he will seek in his work only the glorification of God.

This popularity is a clear sign of Florence's doubts in her own cultural values. The self-confidence is broken. In contrast with the energy and conviction of Savonarola, the artists and humanists of Lorenzo's court seem weak and insignificant. In this sense Savonarola acts as a critic of the whole society. His surge to power implies a repudiation of the dreams and ideals of the people.

In conversation with Lorenzo, Savonarola tells what he calls a parable. He says that as a boy he was taken to the court of the Estes in Ferrara and saw the prince and his companions reveling at table with music, dancing, and feasting. But sometimes there rose above the sound of the festivities another sound—the strange, faint, awesome sound of torment, of groaning and moaning from the prisoners in the dungeons below. Yet those celebrating felt no shame; no conscience was uneasy. In this tale there is an element of something more than the moral indignation of the Christian priest at the fact that the outwardly fair disguises the misery beneath. It is also possible to interpret the joys and beauty of the feast as trivial and superficial because the revelers refuse to consider the reality of the suffering, misery, and torment that exist beneath us. What type of art is it that seeks only to heighten the fascination of our pleasures and yet ignores the forces of pain and suffering? But that is the point of view of the artist Grifone, who speaks for all the artists in seeking to brush aside everything that is ugly, leaving his soul open only to the beautiful. These artists produce work of great charm, but they remain comic figures, vain and absurd; and their products can be only superficial, delicately attractive, and of no significance. Even the ideal of Poliziano to seek the sensitive, aesthetic, tranquil enjoyment of beauty and learning has something shallow—in the end perhaps something ridiculous—in it. It is not only Pico della Mirandola who recognizes the colossal boredom that lies behind this constant quest for beauty and pleasure.

Although the ultimate consequence of Savonarola's work, according to the essay on ascetic ideals, is to reduce the level of man's ambitions, to make life easier, more livable on a lower plane, it is also clear that the Florentine aesthetic, "pagan" ideal has declined from within and that the artists of the Medici court, although they rival each other in talents and accomplishments, are no longer able to make a creative advance. Savonarola is merely a barbarian in comparison with the civilized humanists of Florence; he is uneducated and untrained, his taste and sensibilities crude, but he possesses a vigor and energy that bring new life to a people growing weary and unsatisfied.

In Nietzsche we find an interpretation of this situation. The whole spirit of Nietzsche's work is involved in his analysis of cultural decline and the problem of cultural revival. Mann does not follow any particular Nietzschean line of argument, but rather the whole pattern of his thought follows out of Nietzschean presuppositions. As always, Mann accepts Nietzsche only as a psychologist of decadence, certainly not as an exponent of doctrinal historical theories. Thus, for example, Nietzsche on several occasions praised the Italian Renaissance as one of the great periods of Western culture for its high vitality and individualism and freedom from the restraints of Christianity; he found in it a return to the values of the "noble pagan," which had been corrupted in medieval times by the Christian morality of the weak. The Renaissance meant a triumph for the "Roman" standards; Cesare Borgia as Pope would have been the symbol of its complete victory— "a possibility perfectly magic in its charm and glorious colouring."[25] But, as we have seen, Mann constantly stresses his indifference to this lyrical Renaissance aestheticism and Renaissance adulation for Cesare Borgia ethics. Such visions of grandeur do not concern him. Accordingly he presents the Renaissance at its decline. Even when the Renaissance's protagonist Lorenzo de' Medici looks forward to a symbolic triumph similar to Nietzsche's—when he foresees the rise of his younger son Giovanni to the papacy—he regards it in accordance with the Florentine values of the Medicis rather than Borgia's standards.

Have you any idea what that means? . . . A Medici in the seat of Christ? Do you understand? . . . Let the Vatican ring with merriment and the sound of lutes. Let jests and jollity be the lightnings that flash from the throne of this son of Zeus. May beauty and the arts flourish beneath your staff of power, and joy go out from your throne into all the lands.[26]

What is valuable is not Nietzsche's extravagant adoration of particular achievements of the past, but his whole study of the causes of decadence. It is perhaps most convenient to approach the center of Nietzsche's argument through the concepts of Apollonian and Dionysian cultures that he first put forward in his very fertile early essay *The Birth of Tragedy*. These concepts are overgeneral and difficult to define, but they are useful because in his interpretation of them Nietz-

---

[25] 16, p. 228.
[26] *Stories,* pp. 250–251.

sche comes close to a summary of the problem, raising issues to
which he returned constantly from different lines of approach in his
later work. That they were significant for Mann becomes clear again in
*Death in Venice.*

In examining the foundations of the Greek Apollonian culture, Neitzsche emphasized that its great achievements were created out of
awareness of elements beneath the surface, the forces innate in man
which he called Dionysian. The Greeks imposed a measure, simplicity,
and orderly arrangement over the chaos of their own insecurity. In a
paragraph included in *The Will to Power,* Nietzsche summarizes what
he means by this.

This antagonism of the Dionysian and the Apollonian in the Greek soul, is one of
the great riddles which made me feel drawn to the essence of Hellenism. At bottom, I troubled about nothing save the solution of the question, why precisely
Greek Apollonianism should have been forced to grow out of a Dionysian soil; the
Dionysian Greek had need of being Apollonian; that is to say, his will to the
titanic, to the complex, to the uncertain, to the horrible, had to be broken by a
will to measure, to simplicity and to submission to rule and concept. Lawlessness,
wildness, the Asiatic, lie at the root of the Greeks. Their courage consists in their
struggle with their Asiatic nature; they were not given beauty, any more than they
were given Logic and moral naturalness; in them these things are victories, they
are willed and fought for—they constitute the *triumph* of the Greeks.[27]

The Greeks knew and felt the terrors and horror of existence; in
order to be able to live at all, they had to interpose the shining world
of their art, the aesthetic beauty of the dream world of perfect forms;
in their art and their Olympian gods they created a world of their
desire. In their Apollo they embodied a cheerful acquiescence in
dream and fantasy experience. Apollo, who is the "shining one," the
deity of light, also rules over the inner world of fantasy. In their
images of Apollo there must be measure, limitation, freedom from the
wilder emotions, the philosophic calmness of the sculptor-god. His
eye must be "sunlike" according to his origin. Even when he is angry
and looks displeased, the sacredness of his beauty is still there.[28]

The Dionysian, above associated with the Asiatic, means intoxication, ecstasy; it is the force of irresistible life. Dionysian emotions
awake under the influence of the intoxicants or drugs of which the
hymns of all primitive people tell us, or by the powerful approach
of spring penetrating all nature. It is the primitive—even the savage—
yet it is the force out of which our truly living emotions—and our

[27] 15, pp. 416–417.
[28] Cf. 1, pp. 24 ff.

truly living creations—must spring. Nietzsche suggests that the Apollonian art had not been created to overcome the Dionysian, but rather it sought the control and organization of the inbursting flood of the Dionysian. From this, he argues, the glorious work of the Attic tragedy arose.

In this combination Nietzsche has a vision of an ecstatic harmony of human achievement. His words seem to anticipate the later joyful affirmation of Zarathustra's superman. Thomas Mann is not concerned with this lyrical dream. What is essential for him is that the Apollonian art remains conscious of its origins in the Dionysian. The Apollonian in itself seeks the pacifying of the urges beneath the surface: moderation and form—in short, "the calming of the will." The Dionysian is the excitement of the deeper-going drives: the recognition of the forces beneath—"the stimulation of the will." Mann does not attempt to recall the master achievements of Florence. Florentine art has succumbed to the gradual worship of pure beauty of form; it still satisfies only the trivial ideals of the group of artists around Lorenzo. The Florentines may have achieved a rebirth of the Apollonian ideal; for a while, it is possible, they created a world of beauty and form that corresponded to their dreams and fantasies, but it has now lost contact with the Dionysian, the irrational forces of the will, from which all great creations of art must proceed. Hence the boredom under which the world is congealing. Savonarola is acclaimed because he brings a new force, a new expression of the primitive will.

Tonio Kröger escaped from his disillusionment with the work of the artist out of touch with the living forces of the age by his longing for a relation with the healthy, normal, and "blue-eyed." This desire too might be described in terms of the search for the Dionysian. It is a recognition of the deeper forces of human life from which his work must draw strength. In *Fiorenza*, Mann has stated the issues on a wider and more general scale. Hence the importance of Fiorenza to this study. As he does again in *The Magic Mountain*, he seems to find it necessary to argue the whole complex of the spiritual problems in which he was involved. But the limitations of the theme of *Fiorenza*, as well as its dramatic form, prevent any attempt at a solution. There is no hero, as in The *Magic Mountain*, who can draw lessons from the contrasting points of view. Mann can only present the problems. Although there is no ultimate resolution of the conflicting themes, there is the impression of a possible basis for optimism. Although Lorenzo collapses, he is able to assert an affirmation of life despite its misery, in face of his knowledge of a destructive fate. Lorenzo's achievements, born from the will to overcome weakness and in service of life, are the origins for a "morality" by which we can live and work. The constant search for the basis of such a morality becomes a vital theme once more in *Death in Venice*.

# VI. ROYAL HIGHNESS

Thomas Mann's second long novel, *Royal Highness,* appeared in 1909. Its subject matter—the story of a young prince in a small, imaginary German duchy—caused considerable surprise. In spite of the unexpected novelty of the subject, the story was in fact again founded on the problems of Mann's own life. Criticism was so uncertain, however, that Mann found it necessary to insist, in an article published the following year, that too much attention had been given the political and economic issues and the "democratizing" of the prince. Essentially the prince's story is to be seen as an allegory of the life of the artist.

Professional critics broke their heads on the question of how in all the world I had hit upon this remote and unpliable material,—as if I had ever dealt with any other material than that provided by my own life. What is a poet? He whose life is symbolic. It is my faith that I need only to speak of myself in order to free the tongue of the age, and without this belief I would dispense with the effort of creation. *Royal Highness* is not for me an arbitrarily chosen theme on which to exercise my "virtuosity" and to which my lack of knowledge of the subject matter gave me no right . . . but rather once again I was writing of my own life.[1]

*Royal Highness* was written during the years following Mann's marriage to Katja Pringsheim in 1905. In the *Sketch of My Life,* Mann says that as a young married man he was attempting to explore by means of a fable the possibility of happiness for himself in reconciling the claims of society and the solitary—reconciling the need for human association with the melancholy consciousness of being separate.[2]

Certainly it is only with the allegorical and personal character of the novel that we are concerned. From this point of view the work is a very necessary study for an understanding of Mann's development. Within the allegory is a presentation of Mann's relation to Nietzsche as a central problem of his life. This appears in two aspects: in Prince Klaus Heinrich's relation to his teacher Raoul Ueberbein, and in the contrast between the prince and his elder brother, the restrained and disciplined aristocrat Prince Albrecht.

The suggestion of a parallel between the artist and the prince was already made in *Tonio Kröger.* An artist, Tonio says to Lisabeta, can be singled out even in a crowd. He may dress up like an attaché or lieutenant of the guard on leave, but immediately everyone recognizes him as being set apart and not belonging. The sense of being known and observed, something both regal and incongruous, shows in his face.

---

[1] "Our Princes and We," reprinted in *Rede und Antwort* (Berlin, 1922). This essay has not been translated.
[2] Cf. p. 34.

" 'You might see something of the same sort on the features of a prince walking through a crowd in ordinary clothes.' "[3] The opening sequence of *Royal Highness* has exactly this scene.

The conversation between Klaus Heinrich and the poet Axel Martini is introduced into the novel also to emphasize this connection between prince and artist. In his interview with the prince, Martini expresses in the most direct terms the now familiar lament of Mann's artists. He seems to occupy himself with poetry to the exclusion of everything else; and this is not out of choice, but, as it were, from weakness, from a fear that he is quite unable to take a direct part in spontaneous "life" itself. Is it possible, he asks, that it is just this incapacity that is the testing stone of the poet—that the poet finds in his work refuge from his inadequacy? Martini's poem that won him the national prize is in praise of life. Although it recognizes the miseries of existence—life's evil and cruel qualities—it above all celebrates the joys and hopes life offers, and in particular the pleasures of wine and beautiful women. The poem pretends to personal experience, but this is certainly not real. Martini's appearance is sad and unhealthy, but hardly from too full a life. It is rather the result of the constant stimulation required for his work. He himself does not drink wine; he goes to bed every night at ten o'clock. Without such devotion to his task, he could hardly have attained the prize.

Enjoyment of life is forbidden to us, strictly forbidden, we have no illusions as to that—and by enjoyment of life I mean not only happiness, but also sorrow, passion, in short every serious tie with life.[4]

The fact is . . . that, if I were the man to experience all that, I should not only not write such poems, but should also feel entire contempt for my present existence. I have a friend, his name is Weber; he's a rich young man; he lives, he enjoys his life. His favourite amusement consists in scorching in his motor car at a mad pace over the country and picking up village girls from the roads and fields on the way, with whom he—but that's another story. In short, that young man laughs when he catches sight of me, he finds something so comic in me and my activities. But as for me I can quite understand his amusement, and envy him it. I dare say that I too despise him a little, but not so much as I envy and admire him . . .[5]

These last lines recall Tonio Kröger's relation to the bourgeois. " 'There is longing in it, and a gentle envy; a touch of contempt and no little innocent bliss.' "[6]

---

[3] *Stories*, p. 104.
[4] *Royal Highness*, p. 164. Copyright 1939 by Alfred A. Knopf, Inc.
[5] *Ibid.*, pp. 165–166.
[6] *Stories*, p. 132.

In the same way the prince has to give up all claims to take part
in the everyday business of life—its cares as well as its joys. Mann
emphasizes by frequent repetition that the essential nature of his task
is, like that of the poet's, to represent the people's idea of itself, its
ideal, its dream. Whenever he appears in public, it is a day of festivities; the people put on their holiday manners and glorify themselves
in the general celebration. Consequently everything the prince does is
for show, just as the poet aims only at effects; he has to give the pretense of experiences and emotions he does not feel. He has no day-by-
day occupation to keep him in touch with ordinary life—no regular
tasks to fulfill—and consequently no true relation to reality. He con-
trives only to achieve a successful pattern of behavior to present to
the world. Here again is the hero as actor. The prince has to learn
to play his role before the world. He has seen what this meant to his
mother.

People felt happier for the sight of her, whether it was at the Court or outside in
the streets, or in the afternoon driving or riding in the park—and their cheeks
kindled. Flowers and cheers met her, all hearts went out to her, and it was clear
that the people in cheering her were cheering themselves, and that their glad cries
meant that they were cheered and elevated by the sight of her. But Klaus Heinrich
knew well that mamma had spent long, anxious hours on her beauty, that there
was practice and method in her smiles and greetings, and that her own heart beat
never the quicker for anything or anyone.[7]

Very early in life Klaus Heinrich recognizes the particular nature
of his fate, and fears that his own heart too will never beat quicker
for anyone or anything. Yet, like Martini, he has a deep felt longing
for the pleasures and troubles of normal experience. He is anxious to
seek contact with the outside, to attempt friendships with the people
and enjoy their daily life. This seems impossible to him—the outside
world is completely remote. His relations with the boys who study
with him under the same tutor are distressingly formal. All his attempts at comradeship fall flat. When he tries to take part at the Citizens' Ball, the result is a sad failure. He becomes gay and lively, but
goes too far, gets a little drunk, is ridiculed, even becomes the butt
for the other guests. It is his tutor Raoul Ueberbein who rescues him
at the ball, and it is he who draws the lesson from this experience.
Ueberbein becomes the principal influence on Klaus Heinrich's youth
and his closest associate. He insists that Klaus Heinrich must learn
to accept the isolation of his position and give up hope of "playing

[7] *Royal Highness*, p. 49.

skittles with the people." He must learn to find, moreover, a pride in his nobility. "To be a representative, to stand for others, that is something more and nobler than simple being." Such a position makes greater demands on him—involves greater strength of will and character—but this is precisely his challenge.

Ueberbein's influence on Klaus Heinrich certainly seems to have definite reference to Nietzsche's role in Mann's own early life. The name itself suggests a parody of the Übermensch—the superman. The name "Raoul" may also point to Nietzsche. Raoul Richter was one of Nietzsche's earliest and most important biographers and followers, and his series of lectures on Nietzsche did much to arouse interest in the philosopher.[8] Ueberbein, however, is in no sense a portrait of Nietzsche. The relationship is only partly applicable; it is not possible to draw an exact parallel. Rather, Ueberbein is the exponent of certain Nietzschean principles that have been of importance to Mann but that he is now able to treat lightly. This will become clear if we follow Ueberbein's life. His career has been marked by toughness and a determination to succeed. He has worked his way to the top of his profession from the most unpromising beginnings. He has worked incessantly, without consideration for his health and resisting all temptation to relax into a comfortable acceptance of limitations. In this frenzy of work he loses any feeling for intimate human relationships. Consequently he treats everyone with a type of paternal camaraderie, which at first attracts the prince. But Ueberbein has no power to relax; he is unable to be "a man among men." He is not willing to step out of his isolation. Perhaps because of the passionate single-mindedness of his convictions, Ueberbein seems a slightly comic figure. He finds rather absurd occasions to express his opinions, and so presents them with a certain oversimplicity. For example, he is disturbed by the students' song, "We are all but mortal men." There is hardly need to emphasize such equality, he says. It may be true that we are, alas, all too human, but we must seek to encourage the exceptional—all those who rise above the common average.

"I love the extraordinary in every form and in every sense. I love those who are conscious of the dignity of their exceptional station, the marked men, those one can see are not as other men, all those whom the people stare at open-mouthed."[9]

At the opera a phrase from *The Magic Flute* irritates Ueberbein:

---

[8] These lectures were published under the title *Friedrich Nietzsche, sein Leben und sein Werk* (Leipzig, 1903).

[9] *Royal Highness*, p. 75.

"He is a prince! He is more than that, he is a man!" This idea may once have been a paradox, but it has been standing on its head so long that we need to put it back again on its feet to get an effect.

In the idea of a prince, Ueberbein argues, is maintained the most visible, the most express form of all that is exceptional in the world. Common humanity is empty and boring; we need something that symbolizes the greater possibilities open to men.

"You see, there's no harm in my chattering. What am I? An assistant teacher. Not a common or garden one, in my own opinion, but still no better than such. Just a categorical unit. But you? What are you? That's harder to say.... Let's say a conception, a kind of ideal. A frame. An emblematical existence, Klaus Heinrich, and at the same time a formal existence. But formality and intimacy— haven't you yet learnt that the two are mutually exclusive? Absolutely exclusive. You have no right to intimate confidences, and if you attempted them you your- self would discover that they did not suit you, would find them inadequate and stupid. I must remind you of your duty, Klaus Heinrich."[10]

If Klaus Heinrich is to fulfill his obligations as a prince, he must accept the demands his position requires. He must give up hopes of kinship and fellow feeling, order his life with the necessary discipline. What Ueberbein requires of him is: "Reserve, etiquette, obligation, duty, demeanour, formality."

The emphasis on the will, the urge for power, the reaction against doctrines of human equality, the insistence that greater tasks make greater demands on us, that the higher man must pay for his superi- ority at the cost of normal hopes of happiness—all these teachings point to Nietzsche. Ueberbein lives at odds with happiness. He re- nounces comfort and ease for the sake of his work, and works inces- santly with no thought for himself. This devotion to work arouses considerable anger.

Where was he going to stop? At Director? High-school Professor? Minister for Education? Everybody agreed that his immoderate and restless energy concealed imprudence and defiance of public opinion—or rather did not conceal them. His demeanour, his loud, blustering mode of speaking annoyed, irritated and exasper- ated people.[11]

The sacrifice of all comfort and pleasure for the sake of his work recalls in its ascetic ruthlessness Nietzsche's own career—the "immeasurable restlessness of his longing." Such devotion has the same completely uncompromising character that leads to a bitter rejection of all human

---

[10] *Ibid.*, p. 73.
[11] *Ibid.*, pp. 102–103.

weakness. Hence the radicalism of their points of view and the drastic manner in which they express themselves. Certainly Nietzsche possessed Ueberbein's "blustering mode of speaking" that has never ceased to cause bitterness and anger. Nor was Nietzsche able to relax; he could never be a man among men; his wit and brilliance have no element of human charity.

Essentially what Klaus Heinrich learns from Ueberbein is that he must renounce hopes of happiness and accept his destiny in performing a task that requires of him exceptional strength of will and character. Ueberbein emphasizes this in an expression that is distinctly Nietzschean. Ueberbein loves all those who are out of the ordinary, all who have a noble distinction about them. Of such men he says: "I hope they learn to love their destiny." This—"Die Liebe zu ihrem Schicksal"—is an important concept for Nietzsche. The phrase occurs frequently. The *Fragments of the Dionysus Dithyrambs* contains this passage: "You cannot endure it more, your tyrannous destiny? Love it—you're given no choice!"[12] Again, at the period of *Joyful Wisdom*, Nietzsche says: "Love that which is necessary—amor fati: that is my morality."[13] Nietzsche returns to the phrase "amor fati" many times. In *Ecce Homo* he says:

My formula for greatness in man is "amor fati"; the fact that a man wishes nothing to be different, either in front of him or behind him, or for all eternity. Not only must the necessary be borne, and on no account concealed,—all idealism is falsehood in the face of necessity,—but it must also be *loved*.[14]

Here Ueberbein was able to help Klaus Heinrich, because he thus enabled the prince to overcome the melancholy sense of futility and isolation that overwhelmed his early years. Klaus Heinrich recalls this with a feeling of real gratitude.

"You taught me that happiness was no concern of mine, and you pulled me up short when I tried to come by it; and right thankful I was to you for doing so, for it was horrible and I shall never forget it."[15]

Thus Thomas Mann seems to express what he himself as a young man owed to Nietzsche: the justification for courage and discipline with which Nietzsche provided him.

When Klaus Heinrich comes to doubt the sufficiency of Ueberbein's

---

[12] 17, p. 199.
[13] Not included in the English edition. German Musarion edition, xxi, p. 105. "Critical and personal notes at the time of *Zarathustra* and *Joyful Wisdom*, 1881–83."
[14] 17, p. 54.
[15] *Royal Highness*, pp. 253–254.

principles, and questions if the reliance on form and duty is an adequate standard for him, it does not mean simply that Mann is abandoning Nietzsche; it is only the fanatical Ueberbein whose part is finished, because he is still involved in Nietzschean problems. It might be said that Ueberbein represents one aspect of "Nietzscheanism." His is a doctrine developed out of the more provocative elements in Nietzsche's teachings. His devotion to work recalls the dedication of the "ascetic priest" Savonarola; all lesser pleasures are sacrificed in overwhelming submission to the will to power. We suspect that in Ueberbein's ambition there is the hidden knowledge that he too would rather "will nothingness than not will at all." There is a weakness concealed in this devoted work of which Ueberbein is almost aware. Though he is a priest in the service of a greater life, his work has no contact with life outside; we come to realize that his ruthless concentration and his ideal of human greatness are in fact an escape from life as it is, an escape from his own consciousness of the fact that his life has no meaning. And there may be some implication here that the origin of Nietzsche's superman has its source in a similar reaction on Nietzsche's part against his own personal fate. There is certainly much evidence in Nietzsche to support this—for example, the unequivocal statements made in a letter to Erwin Rohde on July 15th, 1882, at the time he was writing the second part of *Thus Spake Zarathustra,* and the time of the origin of his theory of the "eternal recurrence."

Now I have my own study plan and behind it my own secret goal to which my further life is devoted,—life is too difficult for me if I don't live in the grand style,—I say this in confidence, my old comrade. Without a goal which I did not consider inexpressibly important I would not have kept myself aloft in the light above the black floods! That is my only excuse for the kind of literature I have been producing since 1876; it is my recipe and my self-concocted medicine against the weariness of life. What years they have been! What miserable suffering! What inward strife, upheaval, and loneliness! Who has had to endure as much as I? Certainly not Leopardi! And if I now stand above it all with the blithe confidence of the victor, laden with weighty new plans—and as I know myself, with the prospect of new and heavier and still more personal sufferings and tragedies in store, and yet with the courage to endure them!—then no-one has the right to blame me if I value my medicine highly. "Mihi ipsi scripsi"—that is how it stands.[16]

There are, however, no grounds for a development of this parallel. What is clear is that Ueberbein has not established a valid basis for life beyond his knowledge of despair in the way that Mann's heroes

---

[16] *Gesammelte Briefe,* vol. 2, pp. 566–567.

struggle to establish one. His consequent insecurity is expressed in the violence of his opinions and actions. This is the explanation, it is to be supposed, of Ueberbein's sudden and unexpected collapse. As a result of an unfortunate but not particularly important setback, Ueberbein falls into despair and commits suicide. This collapse also suggests a reference to Nietzsche. Ueberbein goes insane in a painful outburst of his personality similar to that revealed in Nietzsche's last hysterical writings. As throughout, it must be appreciated that the psychology of Ueberbein is itself interpreted in Nietzschean terms; his doctrine of superior man and his collapse both parallel Nietzsche's own life, but they are also understood as Nietzsche would have understood them.

The news of Ueberbein's death reaches Klaus Heinrich on the very day when the prince's forthcoming wedding is announced. This fact seems to imply that Ueberbein's collapse is the direct result of his failure to achieve a meaningful and valid human relationship. The prince's bride Imma Spoelmann, the American millionaire's daughter, has recognized in her straightforward, "Anglo-Saxon" way that his apparent strength of character is false, that his overconfident speeches disguise an inner weakness. " 'He may swagger about the place; but he lacks reserve and inner support, and that means that he will come to a bad end.' "[17]

An understanding of the particular nature of Klaus Heinrich's solution requires the examination of his character in contrast with that of his older brother Albrecht.[18] Whereas Klaus Heinrich, under Ueberbein's guidance, has found some satisfaction as a princely play actor representing his people, Albrecht despises such a farce. Albrecht, in contrast to his brother, is self-contained, but only out of a profound pessimism. He restrains his feelings, but on the one occasion when he reveals them he betrays his sense of the bitter futility of his life. He insists to Klaus Heinrich on the entire lack of real values behind the formalism of their duties as "constitutional" rulers. Albrecht compares his activities with the behavior of a harmless idiot at the railroad station who gives the signal to the engineer for each train to depart:

"But Fimmelgottlieb deludes himself into thinking that his waving sends the

---

[17] *Royal Highness*, p. 241.

[18] Hermann Weigand (in "Der symbolisch-autobiographische Gehalt von Thomas Manns Romandichtung 'Königliche Hoheit,' " in *Publications of the Modern Language Society of America*, September, 1931) suggests that Albrecht is a portrait of Thomas Mann's older brother Heinrich. This is perhaps not altogether justified in view of the symbolic importance of Albrecht as a contrast to Klaus Heinrich, but the suggestion emphasizes the autobiographical nature of the novel.

train off. That's like me. I wave and the train starts. But it would start without me, and my waving makes no difference, it's mere silly show. I'm sick of it ... "[19]

Klaus Heinrich is more easygoing; he recognizes the inherent danger of the pure formalism of their lives, but in reply he suggests the value of their task in representing the people's ideal. Once again the passage seems to refer to the task of the author as much as that of the prince.

"And if the people cry 'Hurrah!' when they see me, they must know why they do so and my life must have some 'raison d'être' although I am prevented from playing any serious part in anything, as you so admirably express it. And you're quite justified too. You wave to order, because the people wish you to wave, and if you do not really control their wishes and aspirations, yet you express them and give them substance, and may be that's no slight matter."[20]

The true reason for Klaus Heinrich's optimism that he can find a solution lies in his kinship with the people. This distinguishes him from his brother. Albrecht has delicate, refined features. He has none of the characteristics of his subjects, and at bottom he has a real contempt for them. This is not, he says, from "aristocratic feelings"— the very idea of human superiority seems an absurd and pitiful thing—but rather because he is entirely unconcerned with their problems; he cannot consider himself as their representative, nor does he wish to represent anything more than himself. Klaus Heinrich, in contrast, has much in common with the people. He shares the same racial features—fair hair, broad, high cheek bones, and deep-set eyes. It is in him that the people have always felt themselves to be represented. He is always greeted with great enthusiasm, while his brother's appearance in public does not arouse any responsive feeling.

Albrecht denies having any sense of aristocratic superiority, but for all that there is a very definite element of the "noble" in his character. The word "vornehm" is constantly used to describe him. As a boy Klaus Heinrich always considers his older brother "the nobler," and suspects that Albrecht despises him. Whereas Klaus Heinrich is somewhat soft, easily controlled, and easily moved to tears, the young Albrecht is self-sufficient and never cries. He has often been sick and and seen death "face to face," and learned not to expect much of the world. "But Albrecht had faced Death, yet never cried on any condition. He stuck his short, rounded underlip a little forward, and sucked it lightly against the upper one—that was all. He was most superior."[21]

[19] *Royal Highness*, p. 132.
[20] *Ibid.*, p. 133.
[21] *Ibid.*, p. 43.

There is something of the Nietzschean then in Albrecht too, as this emphasis on "nobility" and the use of the term "vornehm" suggests. His nobility lies in his capacity for feeling and suffering, in his proud withdrawal, in his distaste for the vulgarity of the people, in his contempt for illusions that seem hardly worth believing in. Alongside his superiority, Ueberbein's overwork and indecent enthusiasm appear vulgar and absurd.

A number of examples of Albrecht's phraseology seem to recall favorite turns of expression in Nietzsche, and thus point up the relationship. Speaking of popularity with the people, for example, Albrecht says: "This kind of happiness smells unpleasant, it seems to me." It is characteristic of Nietzsche to describe the evil smell that betrays the real nature of our search for comfortable happiness or ideals built out of falsehood. Compare, for example, a passage in the *Genealogy of Morals:* "I can endure it no longer. Bad air! Bad air! These workshops *where ideals are manufactured*—verily they reek with the crassest lies."[22] Then too, more than once Albrecht uses the favorite Nietzschean phrase "without shame." "To carry off all the flummery of highness without any feeling of shame."[23] And there is the idiom "That is my kind of ... " ("Das ist meine Art von ... "): "That is my kind of friendliness to the people."[24] Albrecht is speaking of the ridiculousness of human pretense to nobility, and then makes a paradoxical application of this to "friendliness to the people," in the same manner as Nietzsche introduces a new and paradoxical element into an accepted mode of thought.

Albrecht's "nobility," however, really betrays decadence in the Nietzschean sense. He has no power of the will, no drive to self-assertion. For example, a striking passage in the second paragraph of the section "What is noble?" in *Beyond Good and Evil,* applies all too clearly to Albrecht. The aristocracy in France at the time of the revolution, Nietzsche says, betrayed its corruption in nothing more clearly than the way in which it threw away its privileges with sublime disgust for the vulgarity of power. For this was exactly the denial of all positive values—it was acquiescence in the principle of dissolution and decay. The essential thing in an aristocracy is that it should accept its position as master with a good conscience, avoid any sentimental weakness, and accept even the sacrifice of other individuals who for the sake of the aristocracy may have to be suppressed

---

[22] 13, p. 49.
[23] *Royal Highness*, p. 134.
[24] *Ibid.*

and reduced to incomplete men.[25] Albrecht's overrefinement and superiority of taste includes no force that will resist the urge to decay. Mann is as conscious as Nietzsche of the need for resistance to this aristocratic self-denial.

In contrast to Albrecht, Klaus Heinrich has always felt a close kinship with the ordinary people and a longing to share their lives. This is his salvation; although it has caused him to suffer all the more from his isolation, it gives a meaning to his position as their representative. Here Mann seems humorously to be relating himself to the people, emphasizing that contact with the commonplace and ordinary that Tonio Kröger expresses. This characteristic in him contrasts with the intellectual arrogance of Nietzsche.

Under Ueberbein's guidance, Klaus Heinrich had taken courage and learned to accept his task; he had established a successful mode of life only at the cost of escaping from reality. He comes to realize, however, that only by experience of living feelings will he escape Albrecht's fate and give a valid meaning to his life. He has the necessary optimism and energy to seek a solution; this hope of a solution is expressed in his love for the daughter of the American millionaire. In this search for love, the poet is seeking a relation to society; it is an allegory of the artist's constant search for experience of real feelings. It is thus related to Tonio Kröger's yearning for normal bourgeois happiness, the yearning that will transform him, as he believes, from a literary man into a poet; it can be contrasted with Detlev Spinell's rejection of the outer world.

It seems hardly questionable that Imma's role largely corresponds to that played by Katja Pringsheim in Mann's life. One connecting element, the racial question, may be mentioned. Katja was partly Jewish, and Imma Spoelmann has one quarter Indian blood—a fact which otherwise does not seem to have any importance. Because of her father's colossal wealth, Imma Spoelmann is as isolated as Klaus Heinrich himself, and equally unable to fit into any social circle. She greets his overtures of friendship, however, with considerable reserve. She finds in him, as so many others have done, a depressing lack of feeling. In his concept of "duty" she sees an absence of pity, tolerance, and human sympathy as well as an incapacity for direct emotion. This becomes the key to their relationship, and is the occasion for more than one burst of anger on her part.

---

[25] Cf. 12, p. 225.

"I'll tell you something, Highness, and please note it well. If your Eminence is not inclined to show a little sympathy and indulgence and mildness, I shall have to decline the pleasure of your distinguished company once and for all."[26]

Only very gradually does she come to believe in the sincerity of his love for her. At first she responds out of pity—a recognition of his loneliness and his suffering. Later this pity turns to love. Finally, the country's economic crisis brings them together. Inspired by the idea that he can do something for the benefit of his country, Klaus Heinrich studies the economic problem with a real interest in the subject in itself. He at last feels he is taking part, he is giving something of himself to this problem. It is then for the first time that Imma feels his heart is alive, and she begins to find in him a real person whom she can love. They study together, and from their studies a mutual sympathy and understanding develops. Nothing more stands in their way, and all ends happily. Imma becomes his wife, and Mr. Spoelmann makes the country a generous loan, which restores its economic prosperity overnight.

The happy ending seems to reflect the success of the solitary writer's reconciliation with society through his marriage. In spite of Nietzsche, Mann finds it possible to reconcile a "lofty calling" with personal happiness. Ueberbein had lived at enmity with good fortune and out of contact with society. In this one point Klaus Heinrich has left his teacher behind. Through knowledge of love, the poet will gain knowledge of life.

"But we are so stupid and so lonely, Prince—on the peaks of humanity, as Doctor Ueberbein used always to say—and we know absolutely nothing of life."

"Nothing, little Imma? What was it, then, which at last gave you confidence in me, and brought us to study so practically the public weal? Does he know nothing of life who knows of love? That shall be our business in future: Highness and Love—an austere happiness."[27]

The solution is doubtful, however, especially considering the artificial and impersonal character of the allegory. Also, the problem is a constant one, and the relationship must always be sought. This problem returns in a more earnest, more persuasive form in *Death in Venice*.

[26] *Royal Highness*, p. 236.
[27] *Ibid.*, p. 338.

# VII. DEATH IN VENICE

THE MOOD of *Death in Venice* is one of intense and sustained seriousness that contrasts vividly with the lightness and artificiality of
*Royal Highness*. The collapse of the author-hero Gustav von Aschenbach is foreshadowed by a mood of impending calamity, a profound
sense of the relentless and inevitable doom that is to overwhelm him.
Mann temporarily abandons the irony of the earlier works, which had
provided distance and an impression of restrained detachment from
the passionate conflicts in which his characters were involved. His
style acquires something of the academic solemnity with which he
credits his hero.

Mann is no longer concerned with the artist as a young man. Aschenbach is a mature and distinguished author who has made his name
celebrated throughout Europe. He is a writer of great accomplishment whose work has a quality of the classic, a stamp of conscious
and consummate mastery that has brought him universal acclaim.
Yet Aschenbach is the victim of the same destructive inner conflict
as the heroes of Mann's other "artist-novels." His writing arouses
the impression of spontaneous inspiration, but it is in fact the product
of a daily service of rigid, cold, and passionate work created from a
struggle "between his proud and tenacious will and a growing fatigue
which his work must in no way betray." And this fatigue becomes too
great for him. All the emotions and desires he had suppressed in the
constant tension of his work take new hold. He has an impulse to
escape, a craving for release and forgetfulness, and this yearning takes
him with such suddenness and force that it seems to act on him almost
like a seizure. He abandons his work and journeys south, and his
journey is marked by a growing sense of disintegration. The discipline and self-control that had been the basis of his life are sur-
rendered to his outbursting passions, and he succumbs to the excessive,
illegitimate desires that bring his degradation and collapse. Through
images and figures, the story depicts the stages in his decline—his
submission to his own weariness and to the unreasoning passion for
the beautiful young Polish boy that engulfs him.

The explanation for Aschenbach's collapse is not simply that he
has worn himself out, but lies rather in the particular failure of his
work. To interpret this collapse, the reader must first understand
just what has happened to Aschenbach as an artist. The character
of Aschenbach's work and the stages in its development are presented

in some detail. In fact, his career as a writer closely parallels Mann's own; and it becomes clear that Aschenbach's conflict is another interpretation of Mann's own possible fate and perhaps, as in the earlier stories, the expression of a secret fear of what may happen to him.

The moral courage that Aschenbach shows in his devotion to his work is reflected in his heroes. It was the fruit of Aschenbach's experience—the formula of his life and fame—that almost everything of greatness is achieved in spite of all difficulties, "that almost everything conspicuously great is great in despite: has come into being in defiance of affliction and pain, poverty, destitution, bodily weakness, vice, passion, and a thousand other obstructions."[1]

This is the form of courage that Mann's heroes have always demonstrated. It is the theme of *Fiorenza*. The hero, as Fiore sees him, is not the strong Piero de' Medici, but the weak man "of glowing spirit" whose courage lay in his victory over inner weakness. This is the courage of Lorenzo, as well as of Savonarola, of Thomas Buddenbrook, of Tonio Kröger. The characters in Aschenbach's created world demonstrate many phases of this same attitude. Mann discusses some different examples, and adds: "All these human fates and many more of their like one read in Aschenbach's pages, and reading them might doubt the existence of any other kind of heroism than the heroism born of weakness."[2]

Nietzsche describes this form of heroism as being essentially German (a fact that becomes important in the *Observations*). In the *Dawn of Day* Nietzsche writes in a section on the "Attitude of the Germans to Morality": "When a German ever did anything great it was done at a time of danger, or when his courage was high, with his teeth firmly set and his prudence on the alert, often enough in a fit of generosity."[3]

This concept of heroism was the source of the popularity of Aschenbach's writings. It was the secret of the sympathy his contemporaries felt with his work. For, it is suggested, if an intellectual work is to exert an influence, there must be an inner harmony—even an affinity—between the personal destiny of the author and those of his contemporaries in general.

And, after all, what kind of heroism could be truer to the spirit of the times? Gustav Aschenbach was the poet-spokesman of all those who labour at the edge of exhaustion; of the overburdened, of those who are already worn out but still

[1] *Stories*, p. 384.
[2] *Ibid.*, p. 385.
[3] 9, p. 219.

hold themselves upright; of all our modern moralizers of accomplishment, with stunted growth and scanty resources, who yet contrive by skilful husbanding and prodigious spasms of will to produce, at least for a while, the effect of greatness. There are many such, they are the heroes of the age. And in Aschenbach's pages they saw themselves; he justified, he exalted them, he sang their praise—and they, they were grateful, they heralded his fame.[4]

Aschenbach, by "prodigious spasms of will," succeeds in producing the impression of a spontaneous gift. Outsiders might imagine that his works showed evidence of a great power working under high pressure, that they came forth, as it were, all in one breath. Instead they are built layer after layer, in long days of work, out of a hundred inspirations. Aschenbach begins each day with a cold shower over his chest and shoulders, and in two or three hours of exhausting effort uses up the powers he had assembled in sleep. It is in the endurance and tenacity of purpose with which he can hold out under the strain of the same piece of work that the excellence of his achievement lies. It is not for nothing that he has taken the motto "Durchhalten" from Frederick the Great, the hero of one of his most important epics.

This lack of inspiration is the most mysterious and perhaps the most significant sign of modern decadence. Nietzsche asks in *Ecce Homo:*

Has anyone at the end of the nineteenth century any distinct notion of what poets of a stronger age understood by inspiration? If not, I will describe it. If one had the smallest vestige of superstition left in one, it would hardly be possible completely to set aside the idea that one is the mere incarnation, spokesman, or medium of an almighty power. The idea of revelation, in the sense that something which profoundly convulses and upsets one becomes suddenly visible and audible with indescribable certainty and accuracy,—describes the simple fact. One hears—one does not seek; one takes—one does not ask who gives, a thought suddenly flashes up like lightning; it comes with necessity, without faltering—I have never had any choice in the matter ... Everything happens quite involuntarily, as if in a tempestuous outburst of freedom, of absoluteness, of power and divinity ... This is my experience of inspiration. I do not doubt but that I should have to go back thousands of years before I could find another who could say to me: "It is mine also!"[5]

Aschenbach succeeds in giving the impression of spontaneity, a pretense of overflowing inspiration that he does not possess. He has become in fact, like Thomas Buddenbrook and others, the actor of his own role. He is driven on to represent the ideal he had created for himself, and, again like Thomas Buddenbrook, is exhausted by the con-

---

[4] *Stories*, p. 385.
[5] 17, pp. 101–103.

stant tension this part involves. "What? A great man?" Nietzsche asks, "I always see merely the actor of his own ideal."[6] Aschenbach then is again the artist as actor, as Tonio Kröger unmasked him. In chapter iii (p. 29) I quoted a passage from *Human, All-Too-Human* in which Nietzsche had questioned the idea of inspiration in the artist, and had ascribed the success of an artist's work to his skillful and practiced judgment and his capacity for shaping and ordering his material.

This demand for constant revision is, it seems, in spite of Nietzsche's isolated experience, the inescapable fate of the artist of our times; and it is in the courage with which he meets his fate that Aschenbach provides a model for his followers. Like Kröger, Aschenbach has no real alternative; he is of necessity an artist, and the artist reflects in this experience the problem of the age.

Tonio Kröger had lamented that knowledge was destructive, that it deprived man of all joy in activity, and that it led to weakness and disgust. We recall the passage from Byron's *Manfred* quoted by Nietzsche.

> Sorrow is knowledge: They who know the most
> Must mourn the deepest o'er the fatal truth,
> The Tree of Knowledge is not that of Life.[7]

Kröger's achievement was that he overcame this weariness born of too much knowledge and that he established, in spite of the crippling character of his own psychological insight, a valid basis for his further work precisely out of the conflict between his longing for normal, healthy "life" and his position as an isolated observer. His task was to remain master of his own suffering, never to let himself be overcome by the world's torment, still to remain joyful in knowledge, "in sublime consciousness of moral superiority over the horrible invention of existence." In chapter iii, I have shown the relationship between this achievement and Nietzsche's insistence on the joyful affirmation of life in spite of all its misery.

Aschenbach too had turned away from his early sympathy with the weak and outcast—those for whom knowledge and art were a "gentle revenge on life," as Tonio Kröger said—and had sought a new standard of positive values. This was the significance of his story *The Abject,* a work that seemed to play the same role in Aschenbach's development as *Tonio Kröger* did in the development of Mann's own work.

---

[6] 12, p. 90.
[7] 6, p. 112.

*The Abject* provided a whole thankful generation with the possibility of a moral resolution beyond "the depths of knowledge."[8]

A few pages later we learn something more of the contents of this story. "The author here rejects the rejected, casts out the outcast—and the measure of his fury is the measure of his condemnation of all moral shilly-shallying. Explicitly he renounces sympathy with the abyss, explicitly he refutes the flabby humanitarianism of the phrase: *'Tout comprendre c'est tout pardonner.'* "[9]

Aschenbach turns his back with disgust on the sympathy his age shows with the psychologically ill-adjusted. In their sympathy he sees justification for men to trifle away their lives in futility:

How else interpret the oft-cited story of *The Abject* than as a rebuke to the excesses of a psychology-ridden age, embodied in the delineation of the weak and silly fool who manages to lead fate by the nose; driving his wife, out of sheer innate pusillanimity, into the arms of a beardless youth, and making this disaster an excuse for trifling away the rest of his life?[10]

The expressions with which Mann describes this stage in Aschenbach's career recall *Tonio Kröger,* and again point clearly to Nietzsche. The phrase "Ekel gegen den Psychologismus" ("disgust with psychology") is used. Tonio Kröger also spoke of "disgust with knowledge," and the favorite Nietzschean word "Ekel" was one of the particular elements that gave a Nietzschean flavor to Kröger's bitter analysis of his profession as an artist. Nietzsche writes: "Loathing with mankind was always my greatest danger."[11] This disgust arises from the knowledge of the pettiness of men's motives, the "slave origin" of his ambitions. Zarathustra laments: "Whatever is of the effeminate type, whatever originateth from the servile type, and especially the populace-mishmash—*that* wisheth now to be master of all human destiny— O disgust! Disgust! Disgust!"[12]

Another expression also points directly to Nietzsche. Aschenbach's *The Abject* rejects all sympathy with the abyss, condemns all moral shilly-shallying. This first phrase is repeated later, when it is spoken by Aschenbach as to an imaginary Phaedrus. "Knowledge . . . has compassion with the abyss."[13] The abyss is a vivid Nietzschean image that appears time and again, particularly in *Zarathustra.* Courage, Nietzsche says, is born in the face of our knowledge of the abyss, the

[8] Cf. *Stories,* p. 382.
[9] *Ibid.,* p. 386.
[10] *Ibid.*
[11] 17, p. 26.
[12] 11, p. 352.
[13] *Stories,* p. 435.

recognition of the lowest layers of human motives, and it is the power that yet seeks a value beyond.

Have ye courage, O my brethren? Are ye stout-hearted? *Not* the courage before witnesses, but anchorite and eagle courage, which not even a God any longer beholdeth?

Cold souls, mules, the blind and the drunken, I do not call stout-hearted. He hath heart who knoweth fear, but *vanquisheth* it; who seeth the abyss but with *pride*.

He who seeth the abyss, but with eagle's eyes,—he who with eagle's talons *graspeth* the abyss: he hath courage—[14]

Aschenbach has this courage in face of the abyss. Thus he is able to establish for his generation "the possibility of moral resolution beyond all degrading knowledge."

Another phrase links Kröger and Nietzsche. In chapter iii a passage from Nietzsche was quoted on the illusionary ideal of "understanding everything."

At present we regard it as a matter of propriety not to be anxious either to see everything naked, or to be present at everything or to understand and "know" everything....

Oh those Greeks! They knew how *to live*. . . . For that purpose it is necessary to keep bravely to the surface, to worship appearance. . . . These Greeks were super-ficial—*from profundity*.[15]

Tonio Kröger showed his distaste for the phrase "Tout comprendre c'est tout pardonner"; the same distaste is attributed to Aschenbach, who repudiates the "flabby humanitarianism" that it reveals. The German "die Laxheit des Mitleidssatzes" means literally the "laxity of this phrase born of pity." Nietzsche writes: "Pity is the greatest danger." Pity, gained through knowledge of human weakness and human suffering, was the basis of the philosophy of Schopenhauer that he rejected, for, as he writes: "Schopenhauer was right in this respect; by means of pity life is denied and made more *worthy of denial*, pity is the "praxis" of nihilism."[16]

The sympathy with the unfortunate, the psychological study of the outcast, could only prove destructive. If knowledge means insight into the human soul at the cost of our capacity for life and action, then it must be abandoned and a new basis for human dignity acquired. Mann turns to the Nietzsche who likes to repudiate all knowledge that does not serve life, who insists that the search for hidden truth

[14] 11, p. 353.
[15] 10, pp. 9–10.
[16] 16, p. 132.

must be subordinate to the need for the furthering and heightening of life. Nietzsche says in *Beyond Good and Evil:*

The falseness of an opinion is not for us any objection to it; it is here, perhaps, that our new language sounds most strangely. The question is, how far an opinion is life-furthering, life-preserving, species-preserving, perhaps species-rearing; and we are fundamentally inclined to maintain that the falsest opinions . . . are the most indispensable to us; that without a recognition of logical fictions . . . a man could not live.[17]

Accordingly, Aschenbach turns his back on knowledge lest it "lame his will or power of action, paralyze his feelings or passions, deprive any of these of their conviction or utility."[18] This was the strength and meaning of his achievement.

Tonio Kröger has accepted the conclusion that although his impressions could not be formulated when his feelings were excited, it was only when his feelings were stirred, when "his heart was alive," that his work could have value. It was only this power of love that would make him from a literary man into a poet. But the artist knows he must organize and control his feelings if they are to become a part of his finished work. Aschenbach learned to bridle and temper his sensibilities by his scrupulosity and fastidiousness. This had seemed to him the essential nature of the literary gift.[19] His sensitive care and precision of thought are devoted to the service of beauty and form. His work is infused with the love and passion he devotes to it. When he writes his last essay at a table on the beach at the Lido in the presence of Tadzio, he feels for the last time and more than ever before in his life this joy and love that he has given to his art, and his pride in the knowledge that "Eros is in the word"; he writes his essay in a prose that is lofty, chaste, noble, and yet poignant with emotion and feeling.

But before this final short period of creative love, Aschenbach had grown increasingly aware that his style had lost its early freshness. It had become too fixed and exemplary, too conservative and formulated. It lacked, he realized, the fiery play of fancy. That fancy was at bottom the product of his joy in his art; and it was only this joy, more than any intrinsic content, that awakened in turn a response in his readers and was the cause of his success. He had become tired and uneasy. The desire to escape overwhelmed him.

What had happened? When the forces of chaos have taken hold of

---

[17] 12, p. 8.
[18] *Stories*, p. 386.
[19] Cf. *ibid.*, p. 381.

him, irresistibly held by his passion for Tadzio and already a victim
of the cholera and close to death, Aschenbach recognizes in a moment
of enlightenment the cause of his collapse. The struggle for mastery
was always uncertain. Can the poet at any time hope to be teacher and
moral guide? Speaking to an imaginary Phaedrus, in the manner of
Socrates, Aschenbach reflects on his past career.

"But, now tell me, my dear boy, do you believe that such a man can ever attain
wisdom and true manly worth, for whom the path to the spirit must lead through
the senses?... For you know that we poets cannot walk the way of beauty without
Eros as our companion and guide. We may be heroic after our fashion, disciplined
warriors of our craft, yet we are all like women, for we exult in passion, and love
is still our desire—our craving and our shame. And from this you will perceive
that we poets can be neither wise nor worthy citizens. . . . Our magisterial style is
all folly and pretence, our honourable repute a farce, the crowd's belief in us
merely laughable. And to teach youth, or the populace, by means of art is a dangerous practice and ought to be forbidden. For what good can an artist be as a
teacher, when from his birth up he is headed direct for the pit? We may want to
shun it and attain to honour in the world; but however we turn, it draws us still.
So, then, since knowledge might destroy us, we will have none of it. For knowledge,
Phædrus, does not make him who possesses it dignified or austere. Knowledge is
all-knowing, understanding, forgiving; it takes up no position, sets no store by
form. It has compassion with the abyss—it *is* the abyss. So we reject it, firmly,
and henceforward our concern shall be with beauty only. And by beauty we mean
simplicity, largeness, and renewed severity of discipline; we mean a return to
detachment and to form. But detachment, Phædrus, and preoccupation with form
lead to intoxication and desire, they may lead the noblest among us to frightful
emotional excesses, which his own stern cult of the beautiful would make him the
first to condemn. So they too, they too, lead to the bottomless pit."[20]

In the discipline of his work Aschenbach had lost contact with the
passion and power that must be its true source. Zarathustra, in the
"Prologue," says: "I tell you: one must still have chaos in one, to give
birth to a dancing star. I tell you: ye still have chaos in you."[21]

What takes its grip on Aschenbach is the force of the Dionysian.
In discussing *Fiorenza* I showed that the decline of the Florentine
culture could most clearly be appreciated in terms of the Nietzschean
concepts of the Apollonian and Dionysian. Here in *Death in Venice*
Mann directly introduces the Dionysian as a primary symbol of the
forces of nature that the creative artist can never dispense with. They
are the elements of passion out of which his work must be born.

What is the Dionysian? Nietzsche asks. "Lawlessness, wildness, the

---

[20] *Ibid.*, pp. 434–435.
[21] 11, p. 12.

Asiatic, lie at its roots."[22] The stranger on the steps of the chapel in
Munich, who first incites in Aschenbach the urge for distant scenes
and a widening of his inward barriers, brings to the writer's mind
a passion for travel, not merely to the south and to the sun, but
further—into the jungle itself. He imagines a tropical marshland,
beneath a reeking sky, "steaming, monstrous, rank—a kind of primeval
wilderness-world of islands, morasses and alluvial channels."[23] Among
the knotted joints of the bamboo thickets the eyes of a crouching tiger
gleam. Although Aschenbach represses the urge to go "as far as the
tigers" and chooses Venice—outpost of the East but still heir to the
civilization of the West—it is yet the Asiatic cholera that finally brings
his death. The connection is made clear. The cholera has its source,
according to the account of the clerk in the travel agency, in the hot,
moist swamps of the delta of the Ganges, in the mephitic air of the
primeval island-jungle, "among whose bamboo thickets the tiger
crouches,"[24] where life of every sort flourishes in the rankest abundance,
and only man avoids the spot.

Closely involved in all the symbols that seem to foreshadow Aschenbach's death is a frightening consciousness of unrestrainable forces
that had so long been denied. The Dionysian is the rebirth of the primitive and savage; it is the power of nature suppressed by the tyrannical
need for self-control and social adjustment. It is also the sacrifice of
the individual, Nietzsche says. The subjective vanishes to the point of
self-forgetfulness.

Now all the stubborn, hostile barriers, which necessity, caprice or "shameless
fashion" has set up between man and man, are broken down. Now, at the evangel
of cosmic harmony, each one feels himself not only united, reconciled, blended with
his neighbour, but as one with him, as if the veil of Mâyâ had been torn and were
now merely fluttering in tatters before the mysterious Primordial Unity.[25]

In contrast, Apollo is measure, limitation, control, freedom from the
wilder emotions, and is above all the "principium individuationis."[26]
He is the ethical deity who demands due proportion of his disciples,
"and that this may be observed, he demands self-knowledge."[27] Thus
the Dionysian, which is loss of self, is related to the inward longing
for death. In Aschenbach we see exactly the expression of the two

[22] 15, p. 416.
[23] *Stories*, p. 380.
[24] *Ibid.*, p. 427.
[25] 1, p. 27.
[26] 1, p. 25.
[27] 1, p. 40.

impulses: the one parallels the later Freudian concept of the death wish; the other is the surrender to excess and to passion which will destroy all ethical control.

Plato calls Eros daemon and child of chaos. Love, which had played little part in Aschenbach's life, grips him in the completely hopeless, perverted desire for Tadzio that gradually grows into an irresistible longing. Because of this passion, the knowledge of the plague, which the authorities are trying to conceal, brings a curious elation to Aschenbach's heart.

Passion is like crime: it does not thrive on the established order and the common round; it welcomes every blow dealt the bourgeois structure, every weakening of the social fabric, because therein it feels a sure hope of its own advantage.[28]

Only in the catastrophic dream, which is the scene of his final degradation, does the Dionysian, previously concealed, find expression in Aschenbach's consciousness. Perhaps, Mann suggests, "dream" would hardly seem the right word for the physical and mental experience that burst upon him as if from the outside, and left the whole cultural system of his lifetime ravaged and destroyed. It is, as it were, the last stage in the complete overthrow of his intellectual self-control.

Certain suggestions of the significance of the Dionysian earlier in the story become important in retrospect in the light of Aschenbach's final dream of a Bacchic orgy. So we have the goat-bearded ticket seller crossing over to Venice; also the references to Pan, companion of Dionysus, seem to prefigure the Dionysian climax. On the morning when his passion for Tadzio is to pass out of all bounds, Aschenbach has risen early to see the dawn breaking.

Troops of small feathery white clouds ranged over the sky, like grazing herds of the gods. A stronger wind arose, and Poseidon's horses ran up, arching their manes, among them too the steers of him with the purpled locks, who lowered their horns and bellowed as they came on; while like prancing *goats* the waves on the farther strand leaped among the craggy rocks. It was a world possessed, *peopled by Pan*, that closed around the spell-bound man . . .[29]

But it is in the dream that the Dionysian festival is finally celebrated. Nietzsche described these festivals as follows:

In nearly every instance the centre of these festivals lay in extravagant sexual licentiousness, the waves of which overwhelmed all family life and its venerable traditions; the very wildest beasts of nature were let loose here, including that

---

[28] *Stories*, p. 419.
[29] *Ibid.*, p. 416. Italics are mine.

detestable mixture of lust and cruelty which has always seemed to me the genuine "witches' draught."[30]

In Aschenbach's dream, men and women glorify the "stranger god" in an ecstasy of savage frenzy. A rout of men and animals overflow the hillside with flames and human forms, with clamor and the reeling dance.

Horned and hairy males, girt about the loins with hides, drooped heads and lifted arms and thighs in unison, as they beat on brazen vessels that gave out a droning thunder, or thumped madly on drums. There were troops of beardless youths armed with garlanded staves; these ran after goats and thrust their staves against the creatures' flanks, then clung to the plunging horns and let themselves be borne off with triumphant shouts.[31]

Aschenbach resists, his will steadfast to preserve his own god against this stranger, "who was sworn enemy to dignity and self-control." But the frenzy takes him, his heart throbs, his brain reels, a whirling lust carries him away, and he craves with all his soul to join the ring that forms about the obscene symbol of the godhead.

Foam dripped from their lips, they drove each other on with lewd gesturings and beckoning hands. They laughed, they howled, they thrust their pointed staves into each other's flesh and licked the blood as it ran down. But now the dreamer was in them and of them, the stranger god was his own. Yes, it was he who was flinging himself upon the animals, who bit and tore and swallowed smoking gobbets of flesh—while on the trampled moss there now began the rites in honour of the god, an orgy of promiscuous embraces—and in his very soul he tasted the bestial degradation of his fall.[32]

The god whom Aschenbach hoped to preserve against this stranger god can be none other than Apollo. Aschenbach's devotion to beauty was indeed the service of the Apollonian ideal. He had sought to attain "that measured limitation, that freedom from the wilder emotions, that philosophical calmness of the sculptor-god," that Nietzsche ascribes to the disciples of Apollo.[33] In Apollo, Nietzsche says, the Greeks worshiped the god of all shaping energies, the world of form and beauty, the deity of light, who rules over the inner world of fantasies. He is the symbol of the arts through which life is made possible and worth living.

At first Aschenbach sees in Tadzio the Apollonian ideal, beauty such as is found in the highest work of Greek art. "His face recalled the noblest moment of Greek sculpture—pale, with a sweet reserve, with

---

[30] 1, p. 30.
[31] *Stories*, pp. 430–431.
[32] *Ibid.*, p. 431.
[33] 1, p. 22.

clustering honey-coloured ringlets, the brow and nose descending in one line, the winning mouth, the expression of pure and godlike serenity."[34] His easy grace, his self-respecting dignity, and his aristocratic sense of duty and obligation also point to the "noble simplicity and calm greatness" of the Greek ideal. As Aschenbach learns to love every line and pose of the boy's body as it is outlined against the sea and sky, he reflects on the precision of thought, the discipline of mind expressed in this very perfection of form.

And yet the pure, strong will which had laboured in darkness and succeeded in bringing this godlike work of art to the light of day—was it not known and familiar to him, the artist? Was not the same force at work in himself when he strove in cold fury to liberate from the marble mass of language the slender forms of his art which he saw with the eye of his mind and which would body forth to men as the mirror and image of spiritual beauty?[35]

But love and beauty have deeper roots. What is the Apollonian beauty worth that seeks to live without Dionysus?

On those days when he had seen the dawn breaking and the forces of Pan seemed to possess his world, Aschenbach would see Tadzio as Hyacinthus, the innocent victim doomed to die because he was loved by the two gods Apollo and Zephyrus. Aschenbach felt with Zephyrus the pangs of jealousy when he saw Apollo playing with the beautiful boy. "He watched the discus, guided by torturing jealousy, strike the beloved head; paled as he received the broken body in his arms, and saw the flower spring up, watered by that sweet blood and signed for-evermore with his lament."[36] His love turns to frenzy, primitive thoughts blaze up in him, his mind is in travail, his composure lost. Tadzio is no longer the ideal of ordered beauty, but the object of the irresistible, incomprehensible passion and ecstasy that brings Aschenbach's destruction.

Aschenbach's craving for release is first expressed in a vision of the East, the tropical marshland, the jungle. Unwilling, however, to undertake so long and difficult a journey, he happily recognizes the natural goal he should choose. "When one wanted to arrive over night at the incomparable, the fabulous, the like-nothing-else-in-the-world, where was it one went?" Venice is the outpost of the East, "half Byzantium, half Bruges," flower of the Italian Renaissance and yet in contact with Asia; it is a city of mystical longing and romantic expansiveness—the natural complement to Florence, which is purely

[34] *Stories*, p. 396.
[35] *Ibid.*, pp. 411–412.
[36] *Ibid.*, p. 416.

rational and Western. A strange combination of sea and land, built on tepid, miasmic swamps, it is another symbol of the conflicting passions in Aschenbach's own soul.

The city of Venice plays a significant role in German literature. The opening lines of one of Platen's Venetian poems bring into relation Venice, beauty, and death.

> Wer die Schönheit angeschaut mit Augen,
> Ist dem Tode schon anheimgegeben,
> Wird für keinen Dienst der Erde taugen...

(He who has seen true beauty is already yielded up to death, is fit for no task more on earth.)

This poem, in a way that is strangely prophetic, is actually entitled *Tristan*. And if we are to understand the mood and associations Mann seeks to convey, it is in fact above all to Wagner that we must turn, and through Wagner to Nietzsche. It was in Venice that Wagner wrote *Tristan und Isolde*, and it was here that he died—the "hallowed hour" as Nietzsche called it.[37]

What Venice meant for Nietzsche himself has been shown by Ernst Bertram.[38] "Venice is after all the only city I love," Nietzsche wrote to his friend Gersdorff in April, 1885.[39] Bertram relates what Nietzsche says of *Tristan*, in the fourth essay of his *Thoughts Out of Season*, to Nietzsche's love for Venice. Venice and *Tristan* convey a similar mood for Nietzsche; it is this mood that Mann seeks to represent in the city.

Tristan—the real "opus metaphysicum" of all art, a work upon which rests the broken look of a dying man with his insatiable and sweet craving for the secrets of night and death, far away from life which throws a horribly spectral morning light, sharply, upon all that is evil, delusive, and sundering. . . . A drama . . . in harmony with the secret of which it treats—lying dead in the midst of life, being one in two.[40]

Music and Venice seem one. On another occasion Nietzsche wrote:

And when I say beyond the Alps, all I really mean is Venice. If I try to find a new word for music, I can never find any other than Venice. I know not how to draw any distinction between tears and music. I do not know how to think either of joy, or of the south, without a shudder of fear.[41]

---

[37] 11, p. 97.
[38] *Nietzsche—Versuch einer Mythologie* (Berlin, 1918). The book has not been translated.
[39] *Gesammelte Briefe*, vol. 1, p. 468.
[40] 4, p. 165.
[41] 17, p. 45.

In a letter to Peter Gast: "That last night on the Rialto Bridge brought me also a piece of music that moved me to tears, an unbelievable Adagio in the old style which sounded as if there had never been an Adagio before."[42]

Music is to Nietzsche a source of longing for an undiscoverable beauty and harmony. But it is a harmony he rejects as the sweetest form of illusion.

How charming it is that there are words and tones; are not words and tones rainbows and seeming bridges 'twixt the eternally separated? ...

For me—how could there be an outside-of-me? There is no outside! But this we forget on hearing tones: how delightful it is that we forget! ...

How lovely is all the speech and falsehoods of tones! With tones danceth our love on many-coloured rainbows.—[43]

Nietzsche's relation to Venice has a double character. Venice was also the home of his "counter musician," Peter Gast, the anti-idealist, the antiromantic, the anti-Wagnerian, the representative of the pure South in music—the Venetian master Pietro Gasti, as Nietzsche calls him. "Lion's music," Nietzsche calls his work in the poem "My happiness."[44] Also, according to Nietzsche, Venice is the city of individuals, and solitude, and loneliness. "A hundred profound solitudes form the city of Venice—this is its magic," Nietzsche wrote at the time of *Dawn of Day*.[45]

There is one particular connecting link between Nietzsche in Venice and the action of Mann's story that may have been in Mann's mind when he worked out his theme. Nietzsche tells in letters from Venice in May, 1886, how he is forced to leave the city he had loved so much by the oppressiveness of the climate. "I cannot hold out in Venice," he complained to his mother, "my eyes torture me."[46] Three weeks later he wrote to his sister: "I came away from Venice just at the right time; meanwhile the cholera has come into the open and the city is encircled by land and sea quarantines."[47]

For Mann, Venice has the same twofold character it had for Nietzsche. The music of Venice mingles with the sea that encroaches on the town. It is a symbol of the longing, present here as in the music

[42] *Gesammelte Briefe*, vol. 4, p. 218.
[43] 11, pp. 265–266.
[44] 10, p. 366.
[45] Not included in the English edition. German Musarion edition, xi, p. 87. "From the period of *Dawn of Day*, 1880–81."
[46] *Gesammelte Briefe*, vol. 5, part 2, p. 672. Cf. letter to Peter Gast, *ibid.*, vol. 4, p. 249.
[47] *Ibid.*, vol. 5, part 2, p. 673.

of *Tristan,* for the eternal, the immeasurable, for nothingness.[48] Venice is also a city built out of the ocean, the achievement of man's courage, and a monument to the beauty he can create. The glorious façades and the incredible loveliness that meet the stranger as he approaches from the sea are the noblest creation of man's will. But again, there are inner corruption, decay, and disease; and the former queen of the seas has fallen victim to a petty and predatory commercialism. Is this not too symbolic of Aschenbach's fate—the external pretense, the front that can suggest greatness and achieve beauty for a short time only?

All that Aschenbach can accomplish has been done; he surrenders to the infinite that is awaiting him. As the lovely boy Tadzio stands in the sea and beckons him, he is lost in the longing for unity, the immensity of richest expectation.

---

[48] Cf. *Stories,* p. 401.

# VIII. OBSERVATIONS OF A
# NONPOLITICAL MAN

EARLY IN 1915 Mann published the essay "Frederick and the Grand Coalition"[1] in which he suggested parallels between Frederick the Great's struggle and the war in which Germany was then engaged. The ironic detachment with which he presented his theme, however— the air of standing apart from the issues concerned when emotions had risen so high—caused offense on all sides. Although the essay was written rapidly at the outset of the war and to meet the demands of the time—Mann gave it the subtitle "An abstract for the hour"—the idea for a study of Frederick had arisen much earlier. Aschenbach had written a novel on Frederick's life, and had taken the king's watchword "Durchhalten" as his own. Mann's essay may most reasonably be judged in its relation to the earlier works, particularly to *Death in Venice,* as one more stage in the author's search for establishing a basis of human integrity. The transition from the moral problem into the political, and the association with the issues of the war, was too facile and too convenient. Mann seemed to acknowledge that such a criticism might be made. It may also be that he felt the polished form of the essay, the very artistic control of the material, was in itself a sign that he was playing with the problem. He may have felt once more the danger that he was as an artist merely working out his subject—the recurrent fear that an artist's work is by nature unserious—and that in implying parallels with the present crisis he did not appreciate the real earnestness of events. Something of this seems to be implied by the conscientiousness of his new approach. He says that in any event he could not continue to work as an artist until he had come to a new understanding of the issues. A fearful sense of unreality seemed to overtake him. He forced himself to an analysis of his position.

The nature of his development had in fact left him quite unprepared for the war; the political, international, and social changes of the time were outside the scope of his work. The war could not be considered, however, as something external and irrelevant. It could not be explained simply in terms of economic and political conflicts. It had also brought into the open profound divisions in European culture. Mann wanted to understand what Germany represented in this culture and what were the ideals that divided her from the West.

In order to establish the grounds of his sympathy with the German

---

[1] Included in *Three Essays.* Copyright 1929 by Alfred A. Knopf, Inc.

cause, Mann needed to relate the issues of the war to his own significant experience. No other form of approach would be valid for him. In examining the spiritual and intellectual origins of his work, he might understand its roots in German culture. He sought to explain his own development historically—that is, to discover to what extent his experiences would serve to explain the circumstances of his age. It was essential for Mann to extend his personal problems into universal ones; the deliberate introduction of Nietzschean conflicts and Nietzschean phraseology into his works was itself a means to show the cultural implications inherent in the form that his own personal problems had taken. "What is a poet?" he had asked in an article on *Royal Highness*. "He whose life is symbolic."[2] His work had a value only because in presenting his own life he also put into words the unformulated emotions of his fellow men. Now in returning to an analysis of his own work and his own sources, he tried to broaden the implications of his writings and relate them to the vast questions raised by the war. The war, he said, was for the Germans another step toward self-knowledge, and he gave as a motto to his book a phrase from Goèthe's *Torquato Tasso:* "Understand yourself! Recognize what you are." He sought once again a feeling of solidarity with his time, but this had to be achieved very consciously and on an all-inclusive scale. As he said, he tried in fact to feel alive within him the direction of the whole culture.

The result was an essay of more than six hundred pages written with great difficulty during the years from 1915 to 1917 with a feeling of oppression he had never previously experienced, with a sense of complete uncertainty in what he was doing. He was working for the first time without the limitations of a set theme, and he was tormented by the effort of finding correlations and connecting ties in all the confusion of experience and on all levels. It was, as he said in the introduction to a later edition, an undertaking without hope of success, an attempt to swallow the whole universe.[3]

At the same time, Mann had to present his own opinions without an intermediary; he could not stand behind his characters and let them speak. The result was a desperate effort to get at the complete truth, which gave his arguments a varied character, sometimes convincing and impressive, sometimes trite or facile. He was never master of the whole material; he seemed to work in the air without too much sense

---

[2] Reprinted in *Rede und Antwort*, this essay has not been translated.

[3] *Observations* (Berlin, 1922), p. xv. This work has not been translated. All references are to this German edition.

of a unified whole. He has a tendency also to carry out an argument logically to extremes, as if for its own sake, or as it might be presented by someone else, in much the same way as the characters in his novels develop their own representative points of view. Later Mann will come back to the argument from another aspect, and will not accept as granted the conclusions he had previously reached. There are many other difficulties to an examination of this work. The changes in mood are very sharp; at one time he is moderate and restrained, another time he writes in the tone of emotional wartime propaganda. Many of the arguments seem to be part of a personal quarrel. After the work had begun, Thomas' brother Heinrich Mann published an essay on Émile Zola that avoided the censor by apparently dealing with the issues of the Dreyfus case but that was in fact a brilliant attack on Germany's reactionary militarism. This essay—and to some extent Heinrich Mann's at that time still unpublished satire on Wilhelminian Germany, *The Patrioteer*[4]—became the rallying point for the intellectual, Francophile opposition to the war. These democratic, "progressive" intellectuals—the "Zivilisationsliteraten," as he calls them—are the main antagonists Mann has to deal with.

The political and intellectual arguments need not be followed in detail, except in that they reflect a new stage in Mann's self-understanding. The essay is not to be examined as an objective study, but as a form of confession; the theories and arguments should be seen as an expression of the inner spiritual problems of the writer. In this respect the *Observations* is essential to an interpretation of Mann's development. It is the connecting link between the early compositions and his first postwar writings, especially the literary and political essays and *The Magic Mountain*. The unity of Mann's work becomes clearer when the origin of his later philosophy is understood to have sprung from his early experience.

The dominant importance of Nietzsche is apparent at this period. "I hope I may be excused if I see Nietzsche everywhere and only him. For in spite of his intellectual and political defeat by democracy, now evident at every street corner, I see still everywhere today the traces of his life and work."[5] He confronts the present issues in Nietzschean terms, and insists that his own position can only be understood as a writer coming after Nietzsche and conscious in everything of what Nietzsche has meant. Not only are the attacks on the Allies Nietzschean, but also his attempt at the preservation of positive German cultural

[4] *Der Untertan* (Leipzig, 1918); translated as *The Patrioteer* (New York, 1921).
[5] P. 518.

values is rooted in the problems Nietzsche has presented us. It may be added that the importance of Nietzsche throughout the work suggests also the Nietzschean basis to *The Magic Mountain*, for all the wide knowledge of human culture that work embraces.

Mann's contempt for the easy phrases and apparent superficial complacency of Western liberalism provided the original stimulus for his essay. His attack centered on England and France, but in part only because it was necessary to think and talk in terms of countries. There is a certain tone of excitement in his writing when he thinks he can trace this attitude of mind to the Allies, and later a guilty feeling that this was much too simple. He is in fact much more concerned with the "Westernizers" in Germany herself: the democrats and progressive intellectuals who were either openly Francophile and looking for Germany's defeat or at best intent on German reform along Western lines. To oppose these men he tried to inquire what "Germany" represented—to establish in spite of all the abuses and vulgarities of everyday German life what traditional values were embodied in German culture, and thus to expose by contrast what he considered the hollowness of "progressive" values, the nihilistic character of "modern ideas." These "Westernizers" were men of letters, skillful debaters whose arguments were convincingly clear and brilliantly organized. But there was also something hopelessly inadequate about them. The Germans in reality, he argued, were not a literary people; it was not easy to present their case, because they were inarticulate and hard to understand, their ideals were not programmatic or readily defined, their culture was "musical." Unfortunately in the development of this argument, there is often that irritating tone of self-righteousness so frequent in German apologists, as well as an unpleasant nationalism. "Can one be a musician without being German?" The sentence might read more agreeably if the word "German" were put in quotation marks, and it is appreciated that he is trying to put forward a counter program of his own.

Mann's attacks on Western ideals are more attractively presented. Here his arguments take on a more intimate tone. They develop as an elaboration of what he had always felt; what he says now seems already implicit in his own early works. When he speaks of what would have happened if the Allies had won immediately, and refers in a mock international phrase to a "Lusteuropa à la Edward the Seventh"[6]— civilized, literary, and gay, but shallow and at bottom dull and bor-

[6] P. 31.

ing—we feel he has in mind once more the intellectuals and artists
of Munich whom Tonio Kröger rejected and for whom art was a pleasant addition to the good life, or the brilliant circle of scholars and
artists at Florence who, caught in their own decay, turned vainly to
the ascetic Savonarola for salvation.

The origin of Mann's position in these works came from Nietzsche,
and he is able now to find constant support in Nietzsche for his attacks
on the superficiality and narrow assurance of liberal doctrine. No one
had more effectively exposed the optimistic idealism of the theorists
of progressive enlightenment or poured such scorn on the inadequacy
of their principles. A passage in *Beyond Good and Evil* in the section
on "People and Countries," to which Mann refers,[7] fits most convincingly into his theme. Here, though with typical Nietzschean extravagance, the origins of "modern ideas" are traced to eighteenth-century
rationalism and squarely attributed to England and France, whereas
the role of Germany is declared exactly to be to resist this depressing
influence. For England and France, Mann asserts, in spite of all differences of temperament, formed in truth a common front against the
Germans.

Let it not be forgotten that the English with their profound mediocrity, brought
about once before a general depression of European intelligence. What is called
"modern ideas," or the "ideas of the eighteenth century," or "French ideas"—
that, consequently, against which the *German* mind rose up with profound disgust—is of English origin, there is no doubt about it. The French were only the
apes and actors of these ideas, their best soldiers, and likewise, alas! their first and
profoundest *victims!*[8]

All contemporary plans for the future are based on the assumptions
of liberalism. What if the philosophy is built on illusions disguising a
real abandonment of positive, life-creating values? Nietzsche struggles with the vast implications of this question. Mann follows him in
reaction against the sickly watering down of life implied in all Utopian
plans, and goes so far as to talk with contempt of the "pacifist Esperanto
ideals of the League of Nations" and of the thin and pallid interna-
tionalism that is a further stage toward making the human soul more
flat and more vapid. In a number of passages he cries out against the
absurdity of pacifist aims, even against the increase of social legisla-
tion, on the grounds that these programs are born of the anemic will
to disguise the horrors of life, the misery and terror of birth and death,
the reality of all elemental forces in our nature. Such plans are in

[7] P. 51.
[8] 12, pp. 212–213.

keeping with our facile denial of hell.[9] It is only in conflict, Mann is forced into saying, that our hearts are tempered; without misery there is no culture, without suffering there is no pity;[10] and he speaks of war as the very element of human existence from which all our achievements arise. Zarathustra's notorious dictum says: "Ye say it is a good cause which halloweth even war? I say unto you: it is a good war which halloweth every cause."[11] All these exorbitant arguments follow the tone of Nietzsche's scorn of "herd-morality." Nietzsche despises the teachings of equal rights and sympathy with all suffering that are the product of the mob; he castigates their ideal as a condition of safety and comfort for all, a world in which there is no pain, nothing more to fear.[12]

Mann does not often argue so rhetorically or carry his point to such extremes. He seems to be writing partly as if experimenting with the argument or—alternatively—wishing to bring this point of view to the attention of his opponents. Nevertheless the implications of these lines of argument cannot be ignored, and are involved in what Mann is concerned to maintain. There is a sense of adventure in the German culture, we are to believe, a feeling for the irrational, which is deeper and more valid than the all too reasonable ideals of the West.

This trend of Nietzschean argument, however, is not normally sympathetic to Mann. It is too close to the doctrinaire theories of Nietzschean disciples—the "Nietzscheaner," as Mann calls them—who took the philosopher's dogmatic assertions literally and created a program out of them. Mann never had any sympathy with the fanatical superman cults or the ruthless doctrines of power. These theorists failed to see the importance of the "Romantic irony" in all that Nietzsche says, the consciousness of the profundity of the problems concerned, the awareness that one cannot in full seriousness completely justify any straightforward assertion, that it is never the whole truth—a sense even that an alternative argument immediately occurs to mind but is deliberately ignored. This is the real value of Nietzsche's work in Mann's argument, a fact constantly overlooked by Nietzsche's disciples. What Mann finds in Nietzsche is the questioning faculty; Nietzsche teaches us to be uncertain, to question everything that is assumed or accepted. Nietzsche never demands of his followers faith, but always mistrust and doubt.

---

[9] Cf. p. 476.
[10] Cf. p. 491.
[11] 11, p. 52.
[12] 12, pp. 123–128.

What Mann hates is the idle complacency of men who have never considered the complexity of the problems with which Nietzsche struggled. That is why their arguments have an element of hypocrisy, as if they alone were humanitarians, as if they alone could see the stupidities of the militarists and the absurdities of the governing classes. They are men too easily convinced, too much in need of the support of definite beliefs. Toward the end of the *Observations,* Mann reaches a very simple definition of his opponents. They are, he says, men who always know what is to be done and where we are to go. When any question arises, they can always find an answer. "Now we must do this," they assert, and proceed to show what they mean.[13] But all that is of value—true culture and freedom—is born of doubt and uncertainty, from contrast and conflict. These literary men need to have a faith; in order to justify their suffering, they need to be in the right. It is essential for them to have a definite opinion; they do not believe they have a personal identity unless they have made up their minds about everything. Yet real personality is born of the capacity to accept contradictions, to absorb the whole.

The importance of what Mann understands by the idea of true personality may be seen in the numerous discussions on art. These men of letters pay constant service to art, yet in effect subordinate it to a political or social role, whereas literature is in the end reduced to the rank of a manifesto. True freedom in art can be found only beyond the level of propaganda, and Mann comes to defend the principles of the "aesthete" and the more permanent meaning of "art for art's sake." The aestheticism of the artist has nothing to do with form or style, it originates in the equal sympathy the author has with all aspects of life. The essence of what Mann means by the aesthetic is expressed in a passage from Schopenhauer, who finds the quality of the true artist is that shown by nature herself.

Nature acts in this way as do Shakespeare and Goethe, in whose works each character, as he acts and speaks, is in the right, even if it is the devil himself! Because each character is so objectively understood that we are drawn into his orbit and compelled to see things as he does. For he is created, just as the works of nature are, from an inner principle, by the power of which his speech and action appear as completely natural, indeed inevitable.[14]

In his work the artist loves and embraces all life. A work of his may well have moral consequences, but to demand of an artist a moral

---

[13] P. 509.
[14] P. 200.

purpose will only damage the validity of what he is doing. Art, Mann says, does not serve to teach man a new ideal—it does not seek the betterment of man—but at the same time it does ultimately possess a moral value in that it serves as an enticement to life, it offers a mirror to our existence from which we draw energy for living.[15] In his dependence on this argument Mann approaches the traditional humanist standpoint of his later work. And he finds a definitive support for this position in all that he understands by Nietzschean "skepticism." The Nietzschean concept of "justice" ("Gerechtigkeit") most clearly expresses this active opposition to set beliefs and convictions, the need to maintain an open heart, to grant equal reality to every aspect of things. And Mann suggests art might be described, if it is to be most praised, as "creative justice."[16]

What Nietzsche means by "justice"—"the only goddess we acknowledge"[17]—is perhaps most clearly seen in a passage in the second part of *Human, All-Too-Human.*

There is, certainly, also an entirely different species of genius, that of justice.... Its peculiarity is to go, with heartfelt aversion, out of the way of everything that blinds and confuses people's judgment of things; it is consequently an *adversary of convictions,* for it wants to give their own to all, whether they be living or dead, real or imaginary—and for that purpose it must know thoroughly; it therefore places everything in the best light and goes around it with careful eyes.[18]

In another passage in *Human, All-Too-Human* he says the distinction between Schopenhauer's "philosophic minds" and others is that "the former wish to be just, the latter wish to be judges."[19]

Although Nietzsche insists there can be no such thing as intrinsic justice or intrinsic right, he equally discards the suggestion that the urge to justice is necessarily a form of revenge or "ressentiment." In the *Genealogy of Morals* he argues that the origin of "justice" is not to be found in the sphere of reactive feelings, but as the spontaneous outlook of positive and active men.

The active man, the attacking, aggressive man has always been a hundred degrees nearer to justice than the man who merely reacts: he certainly has no need to adopt the tactics, necessary in the case of the reacting man, of making false and biassed valuations of his object. It is, in point of fact, for this reason that

[15] Cf. p. 606.
[16] P. 523.
[17] 6, p. 405.
[18] 6, p. 404.
[19] 7, p. 30.

the aggressive man has at all times enjoyed the stronger, bolder, more aristocratic, and also *freer* outlook, the *better* conscience.[20]

This ideal, which Nietzsche is determined to defend through all difficulties, reminds us of Goethe; the relation between Goethe and Nietzsche as heirs to the same tradition becomes very evident in this connection. For the Goethean man is the most specific expression of this cultural ideal. "Justice" is only a new formulation of the Goethean principle that things must be allowed to speak for themselves, that we must always guard against the tendency to absorb everything and become its master. The real significance of Goethe's career is that all experiences of life are to be lived for their own sake and yet be related to the all-sided personality of the poet himself. This is what is meant by Goethe's "panoramic ability," his comprehensive character that seems to be made up of contradictions. It is impossible to say Goethe was this or that; finally we are inclined to say he was all things, because life is all things. Hence the "conservativism" of Goethe.

It is easy for the men of letters to be in the forefront of advance, to be in touch with the latest ideas and preach the most convincing sermons on the need for reform. True humanity finds it more difficult to come to terms with change. A man whose culture is deeply rooted and part of himself—a man who *is* something apart from his opinions—cannot simply accept a new change; he must relate it to his own experience, must live in it in order really to possess it.

It is important to emphasize, however, that Mann associates himself with the principles of aestheticism only in order to make explicit what it is he opposes in the partisan, political "Westernizers." The association is misleading, and Mann describes it at one time as "a game."[21] The aesthete, as he is commonly understood, is concerned with making a religion of art or of beauty. His doctrines are antipolitical, but equally programmatic. Nothing could be more remote from Thomas Mann than the antimoralist devotion to form, the recognition only of judgments that are dependent on taste or standards of aesthetic or aristocratic origin. The question of beauty was never a problem to Mann in his early work. What was important were moral and spiritual problems.

If the aesthetes too claimed Nietzsche as their supporter, it was Nietzsche the Renaissance immoralist and aestheticist they looked to, certainly not the critic and questioner Mann understood, the heir to

---

[20] 13, p. 86. Cf. 5, p. 47.
[21] P. 575.

generations of Protesant pastors, possessed by Northern problems of morality. In spite of the existence of the George circle, Mann associated this form of aestheticism with the South, with the Latin peoples, and particularly with d'Annunzio and Barrès. They wished to make Nietzsche a part of the South and a doctrinaire liberator from moral prejudices. Such views were entirely antagonistic to Mann. He recalls Tonio Kröger's reaction against Italy, "blue-velvet sky, ardent wine, the sweets of sensuality. . . . these Romance people have no soul in their eyes."[22] To Mann, Nietzsche was essentially a German figure, to be understood only in the spirit and mood of German culture—the mood that Nietzsche described when he was analyzing the work of Wagner as "the ethical atmosphere, the Faustian perfume, the cross, death and the grave."[23]

The dominant force in German culture was the "Bürger" humanist tradition. This class did not rise to power simply in the nineteenth century; it had been the principal influence in the spiritual life of the country since the end of the Middle Ages. The consequence of this tradition was the dominance of the ethical, the primacy of order and system, of discipline and duty, over individual temperament and mood. In this atmosphere European aestheticism and doctrines of "l'art pour l'art" could not take hold. Mann's own concept of art fits into this tradition. He denies the moral or political service of art. At the same time art and culture could not be ideals in themselves; they were subordinate to the cultivation of the whole man. The work, whatever its value, is of only secondary importance beside the ordering of our life.

Mann calls the principle on which this tradition was based "the ethical mastery of the craftsman." He looks back to a time, which he argues is specifically a part of the German past, when the work not only of artists but of all men had a value in itself, aimed at excellence for its own sake, just because it was the natural product of a man's life. Perfection in the craft was a possibility for all, not possible just to the utmost efforts of genius. This tradition continued in the German attitude to work; and, though Mann reluctantly admits this ideal is past, he maintains that something of this attitude remains that is quite different from the ethics of the international bourgeoisie, where work is an ascetic driving forward to further effort and has become all too frequently a mask to disguise the fruitless pains of life.

---

[22] *Stories*, p. 110.
[23] P. 572; quoted from Nietzsche's letter to Erwin Rohde, October 8, 1868, *Gesammelte Briefe*, vol. 2, p. 72.

Now only what is produced justifies life; the very existing is not in itself sufficient. The profession—the external achievement—disguises the collapse within.[24]

Mann insists that he is in every sense heir to this tradition, that all the influences that had been important in his life had come from this source, although he has come late on the scene and although the unity and spiritual creativity of the culture are beginning to be lost. He tries to show that this could be seen in the attitude he had always felt toward his work. It was the natural form of expression for him. He had never seen it as an escape from life, nor had he thought of his art as having an absolute value. If he had perhaps in his youth been misled into thinking that the artist might sacrifice everything, even life itself, for his work, that had been a romantic illusion. Tonio Kröger says the artist must be dead to life "in order to be utterly a creator," but that must be understood in its own way. Mann gave all he had to his work; as if by instinct he felt impelled to do it as well as he was possibly able. But this dedication arose because he saw in it the only possible ethical fulfillment of his life. "In truth 'art' is a means of fulfilling my life ethically. My work—sit venia verbo—is not the product, meaning and object of an ascetic and orgiastic denial of life, but it is an ethical form of expression for my life itself."[25]

He is not concerned with the objective completeness of the work, it is only the accomplishment as the expression of his own life pattern that matters. For that reason he works with such complete devotion that he is able to feel that, good or bad as the work may be, he cannot do it better. In this sense his work has an ethical motive. It is given a value toward serving life. His preoccupation with his own conflicts is also evidence of an "ethical" point of view in this sense. When he writes of his own life, it is with a feeling of sincerity that he is expressing really significant emotions that will be of value to his fellow men. He is never inclined to treat a situation or problem simply for its own sake or as a subject for his artistry to play with. He might add that this is in itself part of the German tradition; it is not chance that the "novel of education"—the "Bildungsroman"—is the characteristic German form of the novel.

Mann is also anxious to associate all those who have been most important to his development with the German "Bürger" tradition. The

---

[24] This argument is based partly on Georg Lukacs, "Theodor Storm—Bürgerlichkeit oder l'art pour l'art," from *Die Seele und die Formen* (Berlin, 1911). Cf. *Observations*, p. 75.

[25] P. 77.

connecting link among Goethe, Schopenhauer, and Wagner lies in
their relationship to this tradition, however much they may have out-
grown the limits of that world, however paradoxical it may seem to
relate their genius to the "Bürger."

It is not only necessary for him to show their common relationship.
It is not simply a matter of discussing the reaction of different men
of genius to a common tradition. It is also true that the particular
form their reaction takes is the most revealing evidence of the changing character within the tradition itself. Each of these men reflects in
the particular course of his career a change in the spirit of the time.
It is implicit in Mann's approach that the only really valid history of
the tradition is in the lives of these outstanding men, for they give
the most characteristic expression of the changing patterns of thought.
Mann does not develop this argument systematically; he is satisfied
with certain general reflections on the implications of his method of
approach, but it is essential to appreciate what he is doing if we are
critically to understand his relation to Nietzsche. Nietzsche too is the
heir to this tradition. Mann very convincingly argues that Nietzsche's
career can be understood only in consideration of these origins.
Clearly, the course of Nietzsche's life cannot be examined without
understanding his Protestant background and his relation to his
essentially German predecessors Schopenhauer and Wagner. But
it is necessary to ask if Nietzsche, as the heir to this tradition, does not
in his career provide the most revealing expression of its inner history.
It might be argued that the extraordinary violence of Nietzsche's reaction against all that is part of his early life implies a repudiation
of the past and even the collapse of the tradition as a cultural force.
Mann himself may be born and bred a "Bürger" and be in no sense
a revolutionary, but we are left with the question whether as the successor to Nietzsche—and of necessity his successor if his work is to
be significant—it is possible that he can still find positive values within
the culture, values that justify Germany's war.

This is all the more difficult, because Mann so completely rejects
the Nietzschean superman cult and the doctrines of power. Mann's
interpretation of Nietzsche is best appreciated when he describes the
philosopher as a "psychologist of decadence";[26] it is in this spirit that
Mann recognizes his own relation to his teacher, for on another occasion he characterizes himself as a "chronicler and analyst of deca-

---

[26] P. 47.

dence."[27] He describes himself as one among many writers spread across
Europe, who, coming from decadence and appointed to be its chron-
iclers, have at the same time the will to free themselves from it—"let
us say pessimistically: we carry the wish for this liberation in our
hearts and at least experiment with the conquest of decadence and
nihilism."[28] How did it happen that such a man could identify himself with Germany in her war and, as the successor to Nietzsche, still
find himself the advocate of a positive German culture?

The violence of Nietzsche's own attacks on things German cannot
be ignored. We see it in the passion of his polemic against David
Strauss. Strauss seemed to Nietzsche to incorporate in his manner
of thought all the vulgarity and philistinism of the German middle
class and all their dull self-satisfaction. Mann wants to suggest that
Nietzsche protests in the voice of the true German culture and German "Geist" when he attacks with such contempt the ideals of the
Bismarck era and its complacent search for material well-being.[29] He
would like to distinguish this new commercial class from the true
German tradition. The argument is oversimple, Nietzsche's hatred of
the Germans comes out time and again in his work; he laments the
narrowness, the petty arrogance, the obsequiousness of the German
character, its lack of subtlety of feeling; he speaks of being condemned
to Germans.[30] But basically, it must be acknowledged, Nietzsche always
writes for the Germans and with their concerns in mind. He praises
the customs of other races only as contrast to German customs. And
his attacks on Germany never have quite the venom that he exercises
against other nationals.

Nietzsche's attacks on the German middle class, however, are difficult for Mann to resist. Mann is forced to admit his own ideal of the
"Bürger" is dreamlike and out of date. He says he slept a little
through the transformation of the "Bürger" into the modern businessman and capitalist, and certainly his eulogy of the Germans reads
at times like Mme De Stael's—it is almost impossible to believe he is
writing in 1917. This fact is curious, because *Buddenbrooks* reflects
all the distaste Mann's family had felt for the new spirit of indus-
trialism in the portrait of the Hagenströms and the implied contrast
between their vulgar and ruthless business enterprise and the old,
comfortable, and prosperous days when the Buddenbrooks flourished.
The mechanization and commercialization of the world play only a

---

[27] P. 171.
[28] *Ibid.*
[29] Cf. p. 214.
[30] Cf. 2, p. 66; 16, pp. 51–53; 17, p. 127.

subordinate part in the story of the Buddenbrooks, yet the character
of Thomas Buddenbrook reflects the new age; in Thomas Buddenbrook is found exactly the spirit that, as shown above, Mann now feels
characterized the degeneration of the "Bürger" ideal into the international bourgeois—the sense that only what is achieved is of value,
the need to make more and more steps forward, work as a disguise
against the fear that there is no meaning to what we are doing, the
complete loss of confidence in life as it is. There is plenty of other evidence of the new world in *Buddenbrooks:* for example, the rise to success of the harbor master's son Morten, whom Toni Buddenbrook
loved as a girl, in contrast with the failure of the husbands so "carefully" chosen for her; or the satirical picture of the new Prussian
school in which Hanno is educated and which is a reflection of the
world outside and the open regret for the old liberal education his
forefathers had enjoyed. Mann had apparently been very much aware
of the change in mood, and yet it seems he had only appreciated this
change as a personal experience, never interpreting it in its social and
political implications. He suggests in explanation that he had not,
after all, been primarily concerned with this problem; his theme was
the change of the "Bürger" into the artist; the change from the
"Bürger" into the bourgeois was something remote and external although it is perhaps, as he is now beginning to recognize, in its particular form a parallel phenomenon. He suggests also that the circumstances under which he wrote his book did not encourage him to see
the new spirit. He wrote when he was away from home, in Italy and
Munich, and he looked back on the past rather than considered the
present. Moreover, the little medieval city of Lübeck did escape much
of the modernization: the old patriarchal system did survive there
when it had long degenerated elsewhere. And although Mann is now
aware that this is past and only nostalgia can bring it back, he feels
he is able to insist that something of this spirit survives. He recognizes on a different occasion that what he is writing is in effect a
romantic rear-guard action, a conservative defense of a past that no
longer exists. Still, he insists that Germany cannot go back; nor can
anyone really want a return to Goethe's world, where Germany was
the battleground for Europe's wars. Germany is of necessity a world
power, and has as much right as any other power to a claim on the
world; all Germans must make a decision. The choice is no longer an
ideal one; it is a practical issue, and sides must be taken.[31]

---

[31] Cf. p. 267.

It is clear that Nietzsche's scorn of the middle-class mind was much more deep-seated than Mann's; and Mann's temperament does not lead him to revolt, as Nietzsche's does, against all forms of intellectual stupidity. Nietzsche, it seems justifiable to assume, would never have taken sides in the war, would no more have been involved than Mann's own later Nietzschean hero Adrian Leverkühn. But Mann is resolved to show there is still evidence in Nietzsche's work of a relationship to the positive German tradition.

The key is to be found in the ethical "Bürger" concept of "life." The Germans, Mann says, are the "people of life"; it is this concept— this "most German, most Goethean of concepts"—that Nietzsche filled with new feelings, and clothed with a new beauty and power, and brought to dominance.

If I were to have to put in a phrase what it is I owe to him intellectually, I could find no other formula than this: it is the idea of life, which, as I have said, could have been learned from Goethe, if it had not come from Nietzsche. But in Nietzsche it stands in a new, more modern, and more highly colored light. This concept of life is antiradical, antinihilistic, antiliterary; it is a highly conservative and essentially a German idea, and in fact, for all his French prose style, his claims to noble Polish blood, and his surface hatred as a philosopher for the "Reich" and the "fraternity spirit" of its founders, Nietzsche was utterly and inescapably a German.[32]

Nietzsche's problem was the restoration of values; all standards and all ideals were to be reassessed in the spirit of the question: Are they conducive to the enhancement of a vigorous and creative life? In order to serve life, even truthfulness might be abandoned. The important passage from *Beyond Good and Evil* has already been quoted in discussing the implications of Aschenbach's deliberate repudiation of too much knowledge of the human heart if it is damaging to our capacity for life and action. The falseness of a judgment, Nietzsche declared, is not in itself an objection to it; and he exclaimed, somewhat hopelessly perhaps:

The question is how far an opinion is life-furthering, life-preserving ... We are fundamentally inclined to maintain that the falsest opinions ... are the most indispensable to us; that without a recognition of logical fictions ... a man could not live—that renunciation of false opinions would be a renunciation of life, a negation of life.[33]

The German culture—Mann says, expanding these same phrases of Nietzsche's—is built on a "life-preserving, life-illuminating prin-

---

[32] P. 53.
[33] 12, pp. 8–9.

ciple,"[34] in contrast to the ideals of Western civilization, which are critical, destructive, leading to dissolution. It is essential to maintain this principle, even at the cost of sacrificing the intimate pleasure of our intellectual doubts.

Mann's attempt at a practical application of Nietzsche's thought leads him here to attribute to Nietzsche a form of pragmatism that seems reminiscent even of William James, suggesting in fact that all truth is to be tested only by its practical consequences. It is difficult to imagine Nietzsche's "free spirit" being led to serve this political end. Another passage in *Beyond Good and Evil* reveals the real emphasis of Nietzsche's arguments in this matter a little more clearly. Nietzsche is expressing his attitude toward the objective man, the scientific spirit of "disinterested knowledge":

However gratefully one may welcome the *objective* spirit— and who has not been sick to death of all subjectivity and its confounded "ipsissimosity"!—in the end however one must learn caution even with regard to one's gratitude, and put a stop to the exaggeration with which the unselfing and depersonalizing of the spirit has recently been celebrated, as if it were the goal in itself, as if it were salvation and glorification...

The objective man is only an instrument, we may say, he is a *mirror*, he is no "purpose in himself"... His mirroring and eternally self-polishing soul no longer knows how to affirm, no longer how to deny; he does not command; neither does he destroy... He is no goal, no outgoing, nor upcoming, no complementary man in whom the rest of existence justifies itself, no termination—and still less a commencement, an engendering, or primary cause...[35]

The "free spirit" seeks a new goal beyond truth: "Where have *we* to fix our hopes? In *new philosophers*—there is no other alternative; in minds strong and original enough to initiate opposite estimates of value, to transvalue and invert 'eternal valuations'; in forerunners, in men of the future...."[36]

Mann goes further in his interpretation of Nietzsche's doctrine of life; he claims it is in the spirit of all the great German moralists and particularly relates it to Kant, to whom he seems to ascribe a similar pragmatic approach. In the *Critique of Practical Reason*, Mann argues, Kant is no longer concerned with the "truth" alone, with the critical and destructive analysis of our faculty for knowledge; instead he turns to the establishment of a practical ethical code for our lives. What else is the meaning of the categorical imperative if not Kant's determination to put his support behind the organizing, constructive

[34] P. 148.
[35] 12, pp. 139–141.
[36] 12, pp. 128–129.

spirit of German culture?[37] The tradition of duty ingrained in German officials and the discipline of the army and its arbitrary code of honor are equally products of this spirit. Mann says: "In the German we have the categorical imperative beyond the deepest abyss of skepticism . . . the will to life beyond deepest knowledge."[38] These two phrases are reminiscent of *Death in Venice*. It was said of Aschenbach that he turned aside from all sympathy with the abyss, all moral skepticism, and asserted a resolution beyond knowledge and doubt. Aschenbach's heroism of achievement, like Frederick the Great's, born out of weakness—the need for order and the will to mastery—is in the spirit of this German tradition.

Mann apparently implies that Kant's ethical code is, after all, simply the arbitrary assertion of a moral law as a false front to disguise the real absence of values. Such an extreme interpretation of Kant's "practical reason" would be possible only after Nietzsche. In an important paragraph in *The Will to Power*, entitled "The three centuries," Nietzsche suggests—though with deliberate exaggeration, it seems—that Kant not only defines the limits to which our knowledge can reach, but in doing so admits the possibility of a realm beyond reason."A theory of knowledge which 'describes limits,' that is to say, which admits *of the option of fixing a Beyond to the domain of reason.*"[39]

Mann's interpretation of historical development since Kant also follows the argument of this same paragraph of Nietzsche's. Mann understands the nineteenth century in terms of a growing acceptance of the hard truths of life. It is characteristic of this century, he says, that it was able to face the world free from the seductive illusions that the eighteenth century required, without losing its will to achievement. Nietzsche called the nineteenth century "honest but gloomy"; its motto, he said, is: "Away from the idyll and the opera." In contrast, he describes the eigtheenth century as "feminine and lying"; it is

Dominated by *woman*, it is gushing, intellectual and flat, but with the intellect at the service of the aspirations and of the heart, it is a libertine in the pleasures of the intellect, undermining all authorities; emotionally intoxicated, cheerful, clear, humane, and sociable, false to itself and at bottom very rascally . . .[40]

---

[37] Cf. p. 152.
[38] P. 163.
[39] 14, p. 80.
[40] 14, p. 78.

The nineteenth century, though more animal and more ugly, is on that very account "better," more "honest," more submissive to "reality," "truer"; on the other hand, it is "weak of will, sad, obscurely exacting and fatalistic." The nineteenth century has freed itself from the domination of idealism. Neither "reason" nor the "heart" commands support. The scientific spirit requires submission to the facts and acceptance of the harshest truths.

If this argument is accepted, it is clear that Nietzsche himself by the very extreme of his skepticism represents a new stage of development. In him the nineteenth century becomes conscious with new force of the fear that truth does not necessarily serve life, that too much knowledge destroys our will and reduces our creative energy. Certain illusions and a certain simplicity seem necessary to life itself. He interprets the growing doubt and despair; he emphasizes that man has become weakened and saddened and anxious to escape. The growing awareness of this clash appears perhaps in many aspects of later nineteenth century thought and action, but it is only in Nietzsche that it is so specifically and all embracingly understood.

This is of particular importance in appreciating Mann's own position. He emphasizes of course that it is at this historical stage that his own work originates, that it is only after Nietzsche that he can present the world so explicitly in terms of a conflict between "mind" and "life." The extreme form in which Nietzsche expressed this inescapable clash is reflected in *Buddenbrooks*. Mann here accepted the assumption as something necessarily given that the sensitive mind is developed at the cost of an inevitable decline in the will to life.

At the same time, as Mann insists, it is the mind that is dominant in Nietzsche. No writer shows a greater intellectual power or more sensitive psychological insight. This is vital to Mann, for it is true equally in his own work that it is basically the mind that triumphs. Tonio Kröger's intellectual longing for the seductive normality of ordinary life is only half serious. It is certainly not Hans Hansen, but Tonio himself to whom we were attracted. It is Thomas Buddenbrook who is Mann's hero, not the founding fathers of the Buddenbrooks' fortune. The perfection of form and style—the controlled irony and mastery of presentation— is itself evidence of the victory of the artist and intellectual.

This irony became the basis for creative work. To some extent the preservation of this last stronghold of the intellect remains the task of all Mann's later writings—but it is a curiosly uncertain position.

Nietzsche's doctrine of power arises from bitter disillusionment. The sacrifice of the intellect to the service of life is a desperate and, and in the last analysis, an impossible mode of escape from his own fatal understanding and spiritual isolation. There is no need to emphasize the destructive and negative character of this line of development. Mann has often enough emphasized this negative origin in his summary rejection of the immoralist or superman theories. Nevertheless, something of this destructiveness seems to be reflected in Mann's own position at this period.

In expanding Nietzsche's arguments he is apparently led to envisage the deliberate abandonment of truth for the preservation of a positive German culture. This is most apparent in the passionate attacks he makes on the modern urge for the most exacting psychological insight, which he thinks is born of the purely critical and skeptical West, and ultimately from a radical will to chaos. What is the strongest weapon, he asks, with which the Western progressivists are seeking their "Esperanto world" if it is not psychology?

Psychology which has always seemed to me as science per se, as knowledge itself. Psychology disspirits all folly and passion, it disspirits life and art—through knowledge.[41]

But psychology is the cheapest and commonest of all things. There is nothing in the world in which the filth of the earth cannot be discovered and isolated by "psychological analysis," no action or opinion, no passion.[42]

Although he expresses this in an extreme, almost ironically exaggerated form, it seems a necessary and logical consequence of his argument. If so, we are led to question whether it is not his position here that is destructive and bankrupt rather than that of the West.

Whatever Mann's attitude to Kant's doctrines themselves, it is clear that he is free to accept Nietzsche's judgments on Kant's modern followers. They are seeking, Nietzsche declared, a return to the past, to the false optimism and conviction of the eighteenth century. *"The return to Kant* in our century means *a return to the eighteenth century;* people desire to create themselves a right to the *old ideas* and the old exaltation."[43]

Mann emphasizes the continuation of this search for a right to conviction and faith continuing into the twentieth century, in contrast to the pessimistic but stable self-confidence that prevailed through

---

[41] P. 150.
[42] Pp. 169–170.
[43] 14, p. 80.

most of the nineteenth century. Yet, is it not true that Mann too is now searching desperately for support, that his defense of the "German tradition" against the West has not become in fact a reliance on the military commands of the categorical imperative? This is a "return to the eighteenth century," but in a far harsher form—to an authority and discipline beyond truth, to the inflexible maintenance of order and control. Mann himself partly recognized this danger. For what happened to Aschenbach was that his concept of "duty"— close in itself to Prussianism and the Prussian code—became an empty shell, a withdrawal from the world that destroys the power of feeling, so that there was left in his work only the rigid service of form. It seems that here, as in *Buddenbrooks*, Mann had personally experienced the most significant spiritual change of the time, but yet not fully accepted its intellectual implications—or at least had not been willing to accept these implications.

# IX. CONCLUSION

MANN'S CONCERN in the *Observations of a Nonpolitical Man* was to gain an understanding of the real nature of the crisis that lay behind the political and economic circumstances of the war. He wanted to explain what divided Germany from the West and what his own relationship was to the German and European traditions. He felt he could come closer to an understanding of the inner conflicts of his age through a new appreciation of his own significant experience, that in his own fate he would find a key to the real meaning of the crisis.

It was above all to Nietzsche that Mann had to turn to interpret the particular character taken by his own work and development. Nietzsche had revealed the reality of the dangers in European culture. He had challenged with unprecedented power and violence all the assumptions of nineteenth-century liberalism, and, had uncovered the threatened disintegration of values behind our comfortable convictions. Mann's own work began here. To justify his own sympathy with the German cause, he needed to relate Nietzsche to the German tradition. I have emphasized the importance of his attempt to show that there was in Nietzsche, in spite of everything, the continuation of a positive attitude of mind that indeed gave force and value to his passionate attacks on modern liberal fallacies. This is not to be found in Nietzsche's fanatical affirmation of the will to life, which Mann finds is not really something positive but arises from a desperate reaction against his awareness of degeneration; it lies rather, Mann wanted to assert, in a deeply ethical relationship to life that has its roots in the German "Bürger" tradition. This tradition unites Mann to his nineteenth-century German predecessors, to Schopenhauer and Wagner and also to Goethe, who retained an uneasy but genuine standard of human values.

This inquiry has justified Mann's emphasis on his intimate relationship with Nietzsche. From the time of his earliest short stories, Mann was conscious of the links between his experience of the world and Nietzsche's. The attempt to find a positive stand in Nietzsche—and hence in the German tradition, however uncertain in itself—must be seen as an extension of what had been Mann's constant search to establish a basis of human integrity in full awareness of the destructive self-knowledge that Nietzsche had revealed to him. The persistence of this unifying thread in Mann's work finally links the *Observations* too with the earlier writings.

Mann emphasized, in the *Observations,* that the conflict between mind and life in *Buddenbrooks* could be expressed in so extreme a form only after Nietzsche. It was not so much in *Buddenbrooks,* however, as in the short stories of this period that Mann's early relation to Nietzsche was most evident. Here, behind the repeated theme of the sensitive man forced to be an outcast and yet condemned for his failure to participate in life, is a deliberate association with Nietzsche's struggle against nihilism. It was not only in the short sketch *Disillusionment* that Mann attributed to Nietzsche a mood close to that of his own heroes. This mood betrayed at once pride in isolation and at the same time a tragic consciousness of decadence. This tortured awareness of decadence explained why the dilletante's escape into a world of imagination led to a life of sheer boredom, and why Friedemann's cautious, Epicurean defenses crumbled so completely in contact with the deeper impulses of life.

When, in *Tonio Kröger,* Mann dealt explicitly with the suspect origin of the artist's work itself, it was Nietzsche with whom he was confronted. Kröger's fear, that it is only the failure who writes, that it is the man who is condemned to separation from the community who finds his solace in art, reflects the extreme vehemence of Nietzsche's repudiation of the artist. This is the Nietzsche who sees the artist as a play actor with a longing to escape into a world of pretense and make-believe, and who finds in his art a road to power, a means to use his weakness as a source of attraction to other men. Kröger's achievement is that, in spite of this knowledge, he seeks a justification for his work. As early as this Mann, with a profound self-awareness and a deeply personal understanding of Nietzsche's destructive thought, was yet able to find a source of strength in the persistent power of life. Only this contact with life gave value to Kröger's work. He avoided the pressure of nihilism, not in Cesare Borgia renaissancism, but in his longing for the enjoyment of direct unreflective experience. Whereas Detlev Spinell escaped into the sanatorium and was condemned to a barren isolation, Kröger—like Mann himself—could tread a delicate path forward between art and life.

This contact with the instinctive emotions of the people was the salvation also of Klaus Heinrich. The prince's life in the petty German court was seen as a light-hearted allegory of the artist's fate. Although other men's hearts were alive with feeling, he was destined only to play the role allotted him. Condemned to be the representative of others' emotions, he has no chance to live himself. The mock-Nietzschean Ueberbein teaches him pride in his position and the need for courage and discipline. But restraint and isolation lead only to despair. The meaninglessness of his brother Albrecht's life is a warning. It is only through a relation to ordinary humanity that the solution comes. In love there is contact with life, and the elect few find a possibility of common happiness.

When in *Fiorenza* Mann turned away from the personal, he continued to extend the psychological assumptions of *Tonio Kröger* and his other works. Mann presented a Florence on the decline. The easy art of the Florentine craftsmen had lost vitality and meaning. Self-assurance had disappeared. The rise of Savonarola betrayed the hidden disillusion and boredom of the city. The search of Mann's Florentines for what was wrong was really centered in Nietzsche's conceptions of decadence. It therefore seemed justifiable to elaborate the main conflict in his terms of Apollonian and Dionysian art. The art of Florence, it was suggested, had lost contact with the Dionysian life impulses it required as its true origins; it had succumbed to the dull worship of a beauty that ignored suffering and pain. Such an escapist ideal satisfied only the minor artists of the court. The giant figure of Lorenzo served to show what had been lost. He had been the true hero, for his affirmation of life had been won out of victory over suffering and weakness.

The concepts of Apollonian and Dionysian forces in human culture, which expressed the problem of the Florentine decadence, were used almost explicitly in *Death in Venice.* Aschenbach loses all contact with the passions and primitive emotions that must be the genuine source of art. The disintegration of his world is the triumph of Dionysus, whose power had too long been neglected. In spite of Aschenbach's ultimate defeat, however, the rigid discipline of his earlier Apollonian devotion to his art furnished a model to the world; for he had provided an example of moral triumph over chaos and the urge to self-destruction.

Aschenbach's work on Frederick the Great and his use of Frederick's motto "Durchhalten" served as a bridge between the artist's world and the political. In the last analysis, not only the essay on *Frederick and the Grand Coalition,* but also the *Observations* can be said to extend the significance of Aschenbach's perilous victory. Mann attributed to Germany a similar resolution beyond knowledge of despair and even suggested that behind the military "Realpolitik" there was an ironical self-consciousness comparable to that of the artist's who turned his back on knowledge for the sake of the power to create. Our experience of Prussianism and the Nazis has revealed the inner emptiness of this German tradition of authority and duty beyond truth. And we view with suspicion Mann's attempts at a justification. There is much in the *Observations,* however, that indicates Mann's awareness of the insecurity of his position. He recognized that the purely German world was breaking down, and that Germany was becoming more and more aware of its relationship to the West. The future lay elsewhere than in the uncertain preservation of the past. Mann partly realized the romantic and illusory element in his adulation of the German. He realized too—in spite of all protests to the contrary, and in spite of his resolute assertion that Nietzsche must be understood as a German figure and within the German tradition— that there was at the same time in both Nietzsche's and his own work evidence of a new tone that had come into German literature.

To have Nietzsche as a teacher, he said in the *Observations,* is not so purely German a source of education as to have Schopenhauer and Wagner.[1] Stefan George wished Nietzsche had been a poet, and declared: "He should have sung, not spoken, this new soul."[2] According to Mann, Nietzsche was more than a German poet; he was a prose writer and intellectual of significance for all Europe, and the importance of his work for the critical education and intellectualizing of the Germans could not be overemphasized. In a sense, what he teaches, what he argues, is less important than the manner of its presentation. An essay like "What do ascetic ideals mean?" (in the *Genealogy of Morals*), Mann argues, is a critical study in form and taste entirely new to German scholarship. In this way Mann can associate Nietzsche with the literary and scholarly tradition of the West.[3] From Nietzsche the "Zivilisationsliteraten" themselves learned to write. From Nietzsche, Mann goes so far as to say, the Germans first learned to associate art with criticism.

It was in his school that we grew accustomed to unite the concept of the artist with that of the scholar, so that the boundaries of art and criticism were destroyed. He recalled the use of the bow beside the lyre as an Apollonian instru-

[1] P. 53.
[2] "Sie hätte singen, nicht reden sollen, diese neue Seele." This is a quotation from Nietzsche himself from the later preface to *The Birth of Tragedy.* "Attempt at a self-criticism," 1, p. 6.
[3] The influence of Nietzsche on the "Westernizers" can be seen in the character of Settembrini in *The Magic Mountain.* As the exponent of the liberal, critical West, Settembrini expresses himself in many strikingly Nietzschean lines of argument and with a Nietzschean vigor and clarity of phrase.

ment; he taught us how to score hits, and indeed fatal hits at that. He lent German prose a sensitivity, and artistic lightness, beauty, sharpness, musicality, accent and passion—quite unheard of until then and of inescapable influence on everyone who after him was so bold as to write German.[4]

The bow and the lyre, as they are used on all the Fischer Verlag editions, have become familiar symbols to the German readers of Mann's works. In Mann, as in Nietzsche, the critical and the creative are united. Because he was himself a man of letters, Mann felt conscious that he was no longer part of the purely German culture, but was inevitably in contact with the West and under the influence of the literary and critical traditions of England and France. Indeed he is the first great German novelist whose work has had an international success. With the possible exception of Goethe's *Werther* and *Wilhelm Meister*, *Buddenbrooks* is the first serious German novel to take a place in world literature.

Mann's defense of an isolated German culture was therefore necessarily an attempt to maintain the past, to hold on to things that were no longer entirely valid for him. What proved more valuable was his attempt to find a basis to preserve standards from his inheritance that would endure as a support in the future. The defeat of Germany did not affect this search. He came to appreciate that all Europe was involved in these same problems. Everywhere the old values and securities were disappearing. Mann's political and literary works of the postwar years recognized the pressing dangers of destructive thinking and illusory escapes; he continued to try to find a justification, however threatened and however tenuously held, for preserving a positive basis of cultural values.

---

[4] *Observations*, pp. 56–57.

# BIBLIOGRAPHY
## THOMAS MANN

The principal references to Thomas Mann's works in English are to the translations published by Alfred A. Knopf, Inc., of New York. The books used were as follows. (The dates given are those of the first American editions.)

*Royal Highness*, 1916.
*Buddenbrooks*, 1924.
*Three Essays*, 1929.
*Stories of Three Decades*, 1936. This includes the single drama *Fiorenza* and practically all the shorter fiction to 1936.
*Essays of Three Decades*, 1947.

These translations are by H. T. Lowe-Porter, except for *Royal Highness*, which is by A. Cecil Curtis.

In addition, references are made to:

*A Sketch of My Life*, 1930, published by Harrison, Paris. (Translated by H. T. Lowe-Porter.)
*Nietzsche's Philosophy in the Light of Contemporary Events*, An address in English at the Library of Congress, Washington, 1947.

References to works of Thomas Mann that have not been translated into English are to the following edition, published by S. Fischer Verlag, Berlin.

*Rede und Antwort—Gesammelte Abhandlungen* (1922). This is a collection of essays, speeches, and articles, some of which have been translated and included in *Three Essays* and *Essays of Three Decades*.
*Betrachtungen eines Unpolitischen* (1922) (*Observations of a Nonpolitical Man*). The original edition was dated 1917. Some changes were made after the 19th edition in 1922—a preface was added, and some minor changes were made in the text. References are to this 19th edition. This book has not been translated.
*Der kleine Herr Friedemann* (1898). This early collection of short stories included *Der Tod* (*Death*) and *Der Wille zum Glück* (*The Will to Happiness*), which were not reprinted in later German volumes of Mann's tales and which have not been translated.
*Gefallen* (*Fallen*), a "Novelle" published in *Die Gesellschaft* (Munich), 1894, pp. 1433–1458, and not reprinted or translated.

### CRITICAL WORKS ON THOMAS MANN
#### IN ENGLISH

Hermann Weigand, *Thomas Mann's Novel "Der Zauberberg"* (New York, 1933)
James Cleugh, *Thomas Mann, a Study* (London, 1933)
Joseph G. Brennan, *Thomas Mann's World* (New York, 1942)
Elizabeth M. Wilkinson, *Introduction to "Tonio Kröger"* (Oxford, 1944)
Charles Neider (ed.), *The Stature of Thomas Mann* (New York, 1947). A collection of essays and articles
Henry Hatfield, *Thomas Mann* (New York, 1951)

IN GERMAN

Wilhelm Alberts, *Thomas Mann und sein Beruf* (Leipzig, 1913)

Franz Leppmann, *Thomas Mann* (Berlin, 1915)

Arthur Eloesser, *Thomas Mann: sein Leben und sein Werk* (Berlin, 1925)

Gerhard Jacob, *Thomas Mann und Nietzsche; zum Problem der Dekadenz.* Inaugural dissertation (Leipzig, 1926)

Gerhard Jacob, *Das Werk Thomas Manns.* A bibliography (Berlin, 1926)

Carl Helbling, *Die Gestalt des Künstlers in der neueren Dichtung, eine Studie über Thomas Mann* (Berne, 1932)

Käthe Hamburger, *Thomas Mann und die Romantik* (Berlin, 1932)

Arnold Bauer, *Thomas Mann und die Krise der bürgerlichen Kultur* (Berlin, 1946)

Peter Loewy, *Thomas Mann und das deutsche Bürgertum* (Vienna, 1947)

Bernhard Blume, *Thomas Mann und Goethe* (Berne, 1949)

Georg Lukacs, *Thomas Mann.* Two essays: "Aus der Suche nach dem Bürger," and "Die Tragödie der modernen Kunst" (Berlin, 1949)

Hans Meyer, *Thomas Mann, Werk und Entwicklung* (Berlin, 1950)

Hans Eichner, *Thomas Mann—Eine Einführung in sein Werk* (Berne, 1953)

SPECIAL ARTICLES ON THOMAS MANN'S WORKS

Ernst Bertram, "Thomas Mann's 'Betrachtungen eines Unpolitischen,'" *Mitteilungen der literarhistorischen Gesellschaft* (Bonn, 1917–1918), pp. 81 ff.

Hermann Weigand, "Der symbolisch-autobiographische Gehalt von Thomas Manns Romandichtung 'Königliche Hoheit,'" *Publications of the Modern Language Association of America*, Sept., 1931, pp. 867–879.

Fritz Kaufmann, "Thomas Mann und Nietzsche," *Monatsheft für deutschen Unterricht* (Madison, Wis.), Nov., 1944, pp. 345–350.

OTHER LITERATURE CONCERNING THOMAS MANN

Georg Lukacs, *Die Seele und die Formen* (Berlin, 1911)

Heinrich Mann, *Ein Zeitalter wird besichtigt* (Berlin, 1947)

Viktor Mann, *Wir waren fünf: Bildnis der Familie Mann* (Constance, 1949)

## FRIEDRICH NIETZSCHE

References are to the authorized translations in the *Complete Works of Friedrich Nietzsche*, edited by Oscar Levy, in eighteen volumes, published by T. N. Foulis & Co. (Edinburgh and London, 1909–1913). These volumes contain the following works:

1. *Birth of Tragedy*
2. *Greek Philosophy and Other Early Essays*
3. *The Future of Our Educational Institutions; Homer and Classical Philology*
4. *Thoughts Out of Season (David Strauss; Richard Wagner in Bayreuth)*
5. *Thoughts Out of Season (Use and Abuse of History; Schopenhauer as Educator)*
6. *Human, All-Too-Human* (Vol. I)
7. *Human, All-Too-Human* (Vol. II)

8. *The Case of Wagner; Nietzsche contra Wagner; Selected Aphorisms from the Years of Friendship with Wagner; We Philologists*
9. *The Dawn of Day*
10. *The Joyful Wisdom*
11. *Thus Spake Zarathustra*
12. *Beyond Good and Evil*
13. *Genealogy of Morals*
14. *The Will to Power* (Vol. I)
15. *The Will to Power* (Vol. II)
16. *The Twilight of the Idols; The Antichrist; Eternal Recurrence*
17. *Ecce Homo; Selected Poetry* (includes *Dionysus-Dithyrambs*)
18. Index to *Complete Works*

References to passages not included in the English edition are made to the Musarion edition, published by the Musarion Verlag (Munich 1920–1929): *Gesammelte Werke von Friedrich Nietzsche*, in twenty-three volumes.

References to Nietzsche's letters are from the: *Gesammelte Briefe*, published by Schuster und Loeffler (Berlin and Leipzig, 1902–1909), in five volumes.

### CRITICAL WORKS ON FRIEDRICH NIETZSCHE
#### IN ENGLISH

Elizabeth Förster-Nietzsche, *The Life of Friedrich Nietzsche;* vol. 1, *The Young Nietzsche,* vol. 2, *The Lonely Nietzsche* (New York, 1912)

C. A. Morgan, *What Nietzsche Means* (Cambridge, Mass., 1941)

H. A. Reyburn, *Nietzsche* (London, 1948)

Walter A. Kaufmann, *Nietzsche: Philosopher, Psychologist, Antichrist* (Princeton, 1950)

#### IN GERMAN

Lou Andreas-Salomé, *Friedrich Nietzsche in seinen Werken* (Vienna, 1894)

C. A. Bernoulli, *Franz Overbeck und Friedrich Nietzsche* (Jena, 1908)

Ernst Bertram, *Nietzsche—Versuch einer Mythologie* (Berlin, 1918)

Werner Broch, *Nietzsches Idee der Kultur* (Bonn, 1930)

Karl Jaspers, *Nietzsche: Einführung in das Verständnis seines Philosophierens* (Berlin, 1936)

Erich Podach, *Friedrich Nietzsche und Lou Salomé* (Zurich, 1938)